The

Perils

of

Beginnings

The
Perils
of
Beginnings

BERNADETTE INCLAN

ARPress
ILLUMINATING IDEAS
EMPOWERING VOICES

THE PERILS OF BEGINNINGS

ARPress
45 Dan Road Suite 5
Canton MA 02021

Hotline:	1(888) 821-0229
Fax:	1(508) 545-7580

Ordering Information:

Quantity sales. Special discounts are available on quantity purchases by corporations, associations, and others. For details, contact the publisher at the address above.

Printed in the United States of America.

ISBN-13:	Paperback	979-8-89356-155-5
	eBook	979-8-89356-156-2

Library of Congress Control Number: 2024914805

Dedicated to my parents:

Encarnacion Esquivel Inclán & Viola Otilia Cavazos Canales

Acknowledgements

This book, *The Perils of Beginnings*, won the Phoenix Writer's Club Uta Behren's Book contest. It's the story of my ancestors, Narciso and Guadalupe Cavazos. Their life's journey illustrates their place in Texas history but was unknown to our family. Learning about the late 1700s, from which this story is told, required extensive research, and I have compiled a bibliography. However, this story of a man and his family is based on the vision and imagination of the author.

First and foremost, I thank my brother, John David Inclan, for his dedication to history. For over fifty years, he has compiled genealogies and family history stories. His presentation on the 600,000-acre land grant that is now the King Ranch inspired this story. To stay on track with the historical timeline I used John's genealogy of our Cavazos gateway ancestor, **The Descendants of Captain Juan Cavazos del Campo.** **http://www.somosprimos.com/inclan/cavazos.htm**

The Phoenix Writers Club Critique Group members have been instrumental in giving me guidance, support, and inspiration. My most heartfelt thank you to Bert Haagenstad, Beth Johnson, Navissa Kaiser, Rick Lindstrom, Deborah Partington, D'Anne Pientka, Cindi Reiss, and Jenny Bilskie-Smith for your shared advice, emotional support, and motivation to re-think revisions I may not have seen or wanted to make.

I cannot fully express my gratitude to my beta readers. Thank you, Cindy Bregman, Sheilah Castillo, Inajo Cox, Glynn Gilcrease, Mercedes Holmes, Sherry Maguire, and John Poole. Cindy, for pointing out the chapter with a glaring loose end. Shilah, for specifying the areas of the narrative that needed solutions, and further clarification on Mexican customs that may be unfamiliar to the reader. Inajo for suggesting I include a synopsis of the Spanish Inquisition. Sherry for recognizing that the first chapter did not have a hook. Mercedes, with her sharp copywriting eyes, pointed out from start to finish many tiny, overlooked issues as well as areas that needed clarification. My special thanks to the two men, Glynn, and John. They read this book giving me verbal feedback on the characters, setting, plot, and conflict.

Finally, there is no way I can thank my husband, Joseph, enough. His devotion knows no bounds. He's always been my biggest cheerleader keeping me on course, especially when I began writing this book five years ago. He knows just how to boost my spirit and energy to encourage my writing—and sticking to the story. Joseph corroborated on the cover with Justice Ink Media Marketing at 602.478.3691 or at the following:

- https://justiceink.myportfolio.com.

- https://www.facebook.com/profile. php?id=61552250164896&mib extid=LQQJ4d

Cast of Characters

Barbara Cavazos-Canales Esquivel – the eighteen-year-old narrator

Eloisa Cavazos Diaz, AKA Auntie – fiftyish maternal aunt

Lucia Cavazos de Canales – Auntie's mother, narrator's maternal grandmother

José Canales – Auntie's step-father, narrator's maternal grandfather

Séamos Manus – Auntie's birth father, a physician born in Ireland, Lucia's lover.

Auntie's Siblings: Fortino, Isidoro (Lolo), Sofia, Joseph, Guadalupe

(Lupe), Otilia (Tila), Genevieve, Alex

José Narciso Cavazos – Narciso, **the main character**. Born at La Hacienda de los Cavazos, in Nuevo Leon, Mexico, and died at San Juan de Carricitos, Texas (b.1750-d.1802).

His parents are José Manuel Cavazos and María Josefa González-Hidalgo Cantú (b. 1728-d.?)

María Ignacia Hinojosa Benavides (b. 1745-d. 1790). Her parents are Juan José Hinojosa Garza and María Antonia Inés Balli Báez- Benavides.

Narciso and Maria Ignacia were married in 1769 in Reynosa, Tamaulipas, Mexico. They had four children:

María de los Santos(dtr) – born in 1769. Married in 1797 to José Ignacio Balli Villarreal.

María Francisca(dtr) – Francisca in the story was born in 1770. Married in 1792 to Blas María Garza Garza b. 1756-d. 1802).

José Manuel(son) – Manuel in the story was born c. 1771. He married Maria del Pilar Balli Diaz (b. 1773). Manuel is the oldest son and heir to the inheritance left by his father, Narciso. Pilar, the name in the story, was an only child of the Ballis of Padre Islands.

María Ignacia(dtr) – Ignacia in the story was born 1779. She married Maximino Cavazos Gutiérrez (b. 1779)

María Guadalupe Cavazos Gutièrrez (b. 1773- d. 1847). Guadalupe in the story. Narciso's first cousin and his second wife. Her parents were José Francisco Cavazos Cantu, and María Gutiérrez Guajardo. Narciso's mother and Guadalupe's father are siblings. Catholic Church delayed marriage vows due to the requirement of a dispensation.

Narciso and Guadalupe were married on July 6, 1793, and had eight children, one adopted.

José Jorge(son)—Jorge in the story was born in 1790. María Clara(dtr)—Clara in the story was born in 1791.

José Blas(adopted)— José Blas in the story was born in 1792. His mother, likely a close relative, probably died in childbirth.

According to family legend, Narciso and Guadalupe adopted

José Blas as an infant. He's in the story as Narciso's and Guadalupe's natural child since I couldn't determine his parents or reasons why he was adopted.

María Teresa(dtr)—Teresa in the story was born in 1792. José Lino(son)— José Lino in the story was born in 1794.

Juan Nepomuceno(son)—Juan Nepomuceno, in the story, was born in 1795.

José Maria(son)— José Maria in the story was born in 1798.

Rosalía(dtr)— Rosalía in the story was born in 1803 after the death of Narciso, her father.

Parents

Don Nazario Cavazos – the bigwig and Narciso's grandfather. Owner of La Hacienda de los Cavazos in Nuevo Leon Mexico

Don Santiago Balli – Owner of what is now Padre Island and father to Maria del Pilar – Manuel's wife

Vaqueros – the following are made-up characters:

Raúl – a companion character in the story. Narciso's best friend and foreman.

Ramón – The cook Ignacio – AKA El Amante

Francisco – Nicknamed El Lobo

Vicente – Nicknamed El Viejo Pedro– the teenager.

Haro - Narciso's onery horse (b. 1742 d. 1801) and companion brought to Mexico from Seville, Spain, as a yearling.

Tlaxcala - Raúl's horse.

Hondo - Manuel's horse.

Indian Tribes

Tlaxcaltecs (Te.lax.cál.techs) – A large tribe whose warriors joined with the conquistador, Hernán Cortés, to successfully topple the Aztec empire.

Coahuiltecans (Ko.ah.weel.teh.kans) – A nomadic tribe who befriended the Spaniards in 1535.

Karankawa – Lived on the coast of what is now Padre Island. Known for their distinctive physical appearance. In the sixteenth and seventeenth centuries, the men were described as tall and muscular, and during the summer, wore deerskin breechcloths or nothing at all.

Historical Figures: Gateway ancestors are mentioned in the Cavazos family history.

King Fernando VI – Ruled Spain from 1713-1759.

Juan de Oñate – Conquistador and founder of New Mexico 1550-1598.

Tomás Sánchez – A veteran Spanish captain who founded Laredo, Texas, and Nuevo Laredo, Tamaulipas, Mexico.

Luis de Carvajal – First governor of Nuevo León and known to meet his death in an Inquisition prison in Mexico City for his Jewish religion and practice.

The Land

El Rancho Viejo – Land claimed by both Narciso and Maria Ignacia's relative, Don y Doña José de la Garza, who occupied the land and began Brownsville, Texas.

The Agostadero de San Juan de Carricitos was 600,000 acres of Texas land granted to Josè Narciso Cavazos in 1792 by King Charles IV, who reigned from 1788-1808.

The Agostadero means pasture and is often used in the story to connote San Juan de Carricitos

Table Of Contents

Chapter 1

A GTO ROAD TRIP

I couldn't think of anything else; what was I going to do this summer back home? My first year away at college was over and I was winding down my stay on campus. I didn't want to leave. I was the only one in the science building busily scrubbing the stainless-steel table I occupied when dissecting animals. I'm the last one to tidy up. *Had everyone else finished classes early?* Only five girls were majoring in Biology, and we each had a sizeable workstation. Alone in the quiet, empty laboratory, I considered my choices for the summer back in Galveston.

I had worked at Dairy Queen the summer before college and the owners most likely would rehire me. *I could probably start working on the first day back.* I dumped the containers of dissected animals into a large formaldehyde vat. The odor overwhelmed my senses and burned my eyes. I washed the glass containers and set them on clean towels to dry. *I could attend Galveston Junior College for that Civics class and get those credits out of the way.* The College was within walking distance of my home, so I wouldn't need a car. However, neither option appealed to me. *There's no other choice,* I sighed and hung the towels to dry. I was currently attending a private college in San Antonio on a full scholarship and wouldn't get funding to remain on campus for the summer. I thought about the possibility of staying in San Antonio with a friend. However, my roommate and other classmates I spent time with were from other cities and states, and like me, did not make decisions regarding summer plans without discussing them with parents. They all went home, so, that settled that idea. Besides, we'd need jobs to pay for an apartment.

Then, as if a miracle controlled the moment, Mama called with a suggestion that changed everything.

★

"Hey Barbara," someone yelled from down the dorm hall, "Reception just called; your aunt is downstairs, causing quite a commotion."

I'd been tidying my dorm room to make the time pass. I shook the curtains and patted the bare mattress. I couldn't help but grin upon receiving the news that Auntie had arrived. *The adventure was about to begin!*

It was 1967, the end of my first year at Incarnate Word, also known as "The Word," an all-girls Catholic College in San Antonio, Texas. My Catholic school education began in kindergarten. However, in the eighth grade, the sexes went to separate schools until graduation. I'd describe myself as shy and somewhat withdrawn— precisely why I chose an all-girls college away from my hometown of Galveston as a safeguard from male encounters—I didn't date or "hang out" with local classmates from the all-boys school. Born with a bilateral club foot deformity that mainly affected my right leg, I walked with a distinctive limp and had to wear shoes with braces attached. It wasn't until my sixteenth birthday that surgery corrected the deformity.

I didn't have to immediately return home to Galveston for summer break. Mama had called the previous week to ask if I'd accompany Aunt Eloisa on a road trip—most exciting news. I'd be traveling with the most outrageous and amusing aunt, Mama's eldest sister, whom I'd always called Auntie. She'd pick me up today, the last day of the school year.

When Mama called, she told me not to buy a return bus ticket to Galveston. "Your Auntie's determined to find her baptismal certificate and asked permission for you to accompany her. Is that okay with you?" I told her yes; "I knew you weren't keen on returning to Galveston for the summer."

"Oh my gosh, yes," I quickly responded, "you're right, Mama; after that humiliating incident last January, I don't look forward to anything going on there."

"That's what I thought," Mama replied sympathetically. "The trip will take a week, maybe two, depending on what Eloisa decides. You know your Aunt," Mama audibly exhaled, "she's uncontrollable. If nothing else, she'll give you another glimpse at her world, *Mija*," she often called me by the intimate Spanish endearment for "my daughter."

Whenever Auntie was around, little of what she said or did seldom shocked her six siblings. She may have embarrassed them, but I loved her unorthodox conduct, her norm at family gatherings. For instance, she told my uncle's wife, Aunt Luz, that when she walked, the wiggle of her *nalgas*, reminded her of a working girl in the red- light district of Galveston. No one ever questioned Auntie on her knowledge about working girls, and Aunt Luz never lashed back— at least in the presence of others. Auntie possessed a harsh edge, however. Some of my cousins complained about her unsolicited criticism about their dress or makeup, but Auntie never said anything to me that might hurt my feelings. Instead, she'd open her arms wide and say, "Querida, you bring in the sunshine whenever you walk into a room."

In a front parking spot, I immediately spotted Auntie wearing a classic silk multiprint dress in eye-popping colors. I wondered if she had bought it at Macy's New York, where she'd lived for a decade before selling the Brownstone in Greenwich Village to move to California. Her distinctive New York accent seemed to have resonated with one of the three people ogling the car; then, I heard her say in a typical Texan drawl, "So y'all lived in Brooklyn at the same time I was in New York."

Auntie loved being the center of attention, and I watched as she sashayed around this spectacular sports car.

Wow, a convertible! I couldn't peel my eyes away from its electric blue paintwork that detonated sparks whenever sunlight peeked through a swaying tree branch.

I ran up to Auntie and embraced her. "Wow! Hi! Is this what you're driving?"

"Of course!" she replied, holding on to me. "It's hot off the assembly line."

She turned to her audience and pulled me close.

"My niece, *Querida*, also known as Barbara." Auntie always called me by the Spanish word beloved. "She's my official companion on this voyage to the uncharted. God knows I require a chaperone."

The group laughed and went on their way. We were alone. Auntie and I wrapped in a tight embrace, and she smacked a kiss on my lips.

Then, she placed her hands on my shoulders and pushed me back with a stern look.

"Do you have your birth certificate? We're going to Mexico, and I don't want you detained as a *mojada*," she laughed boisterously. My eyes bugged out.

"An illegal? Uh, um, no I don't, …what do you mean we're going to Mexico?"

Our family often drove into Mexico, and I never remember having trouble crossing the border.

"We don't need birth certificates, um, I…" She laughed again at my babbling.

"I'm playing with you! What do I have to do to get you out of this place?"

It was a beautiful spring day in San Antonio. The campus was alive with spirited activity as students got into cars or jumped into taxis for the bus station or airport. The campus was a forest of Mountain Cedar and pecan trees that bloomed during different seasons— January and May. Their highly allergenic pollen triggered symptoms that could lead to an infectious respiratory sickness in individuals sensitive to the pollen, which, unfortunately, that previous January I discovered I was one. Our dorm housemother sent me to the emergency room because of severe respiratory symptoms and a high fever. Today, I was leaving just in time to escape the pecan pollen filling the air.

I grabbed Auntie's hand. "I'm packed and signed out for the summer. Come, let's get my stuff."

Auntie's only conversation with Sister Benedicta, the dorm mother, was that she was responsible for me.

I'd tightly squeezed all my belongings into a footlocker, and it took a couple of classmates to help carry it to the car. After hugs and kisses, we said goodbye, and the girls surprised Auntie with hugs, too. Although not overly affectionate toward strangers, she threw them an exaggerated kiss.

As I opened the passenger door, I noticed people pointing and staring.

"This car certainly attracts attention," I remarked.

"That's why I got it," Auntie replied, raising an eyebrow, "it's a Monreaux Blue Metallic Pontiac GTO".

She pushed a button. The top whirred over our heads and plopped onto the windscreen. "These will secure it shut, so the wind doesn't blow it open," she snapped two clips on opposite sides of the windshield. "When we're out in the countryside, I'll put the top down again," she smiled triumphantly and slapped the steering wheel. "Let's get going."

The interior was beige, with the dash and console wood; a metal GTO emblem nested elegantly on the front engine hood. Auntie's eyes sparkled with glee, "It's a distinct model because of the front grillwork and the engine scoop." She pointed to the "bump" on the top of the hood.

I knew nothing about cars, but Auntie, an enthusiast, had a new one every time I saw her. She had an amazingly youthful appearance for being around sixty and, at all times, dressed in the height of fashion. At sixteen, Aurelio Diaz proposed marriage and became known to everyone in the family as Diaz. Once a year, she traveled to Texas from their home in California—over one-thousand miles—by herself. Only once did Uncle Diaz come along—her first stop at our family home. She rushed him in, left his suitcase on the porch, and rushed back into her car, honking and waving. Uncle Diaz shrugged and told us, "I never agreed to come, but she tricked me. I knew she'd do her own thing, and I hate nothing more than her whirlwind schedule when she's visiting family in Texas."

"So, she leaves you here with us because it's quiet and peaceful," Mama added.

Uncle Diaz shrugged again, "Is that all right with you? She said I needed to see Texas one last time." Uncle Diaz was fifteen years older than Auntie.

Mama laughed and hugged him, "Of course! But John and I work, so Barbara must keep you entertained."

I remembered that Uncle Diaz had turned out to be a delightful companion that summer.

—❖⟶⟶❖⟵⟵❖—

"Thank you for picking me up, Auntie. This adventure is all so exciting… And I'm up for anything!"

"I said to your mother, 'Tila, I want Barbara for the company and to help search the records in every small town el Hijo del Diablo (Son of the Devil) took us to live in just long enough for Mama Lucia to drop another baby.'" My grandparents lived in Runge, New Braunfels, Goliad, and Lockhart before settling in Texas City.

Auntie called her stepfather José Canales El Hijo del Diablo. She called her mother Lucia Cavazos, my grandmother, Mama Lucia, or Lucia. I already knew about the contempt between Auntie and my grandfather. Maybe I would find out why during this trip.

"Don't you mean 'son of a b…'" She didn't let me finish.

"Uh uh, uh," she shook her finger, "that reference defames a woman. God knows women are blamed by humankind for every misdeed committed." She continued, "I refuse to call any man a word that smears his mother or a woman just because he's the Cabrón."

Spanish euphemisms are hard to define, especially with my limited vocabulary for words like Cabrón, but I knew what she meant.

"Mama feels the same about demeaning women," I said. "She has a saying, 'Men are harder on women than they on men, but women are the hardest on women.'"

"Tila is a very smart woman. When did that come up?"

I took a few seconds to think; I wasn't sure if I wanted to tell her about a disturbing personal incident in early December. I decided now wasn't the right time.

"Well, a rumor was going around that the neighbor behind us sent away their teenage daughter to have a baby."

Auntie's eyebrows shot up. This was her kind of story. "Go on," she gestured with her hand.

"Mama was outside talking with neighbors, and I was on the porch playing jacks… and listening. They saw the teenager get into a car with a boy and started whispering about her scandalous behavior, especially after the shame she supposedly brought upon her family."

Auntie was captivated. "What did Tila do?"

"She quietly left the group and told me to come inside with her." She told me, 'Their talk about a young woman whom we know nothing about, especially her private business, is hateful. They feel better about themselves when they scorn this young girl who grew up without a mother.' Then she made the statement about 'being hard on women.'"

Auntie looked at me with a warm smile. "Angels danced the day Tila was born."

"What a beautiful image." We were quiet for some time.

We left the rolling hills of San Antonio and took highway U.S. 83 south past endless miles of flat, open countryside. Fences corralled cows and horses that fed off the acres of pasture. I was curious about our family, who followed Auntie to California and asked about Lucille and Julia.

"You know that Lucille and Tony (her husband) moved to Phoenix, Arizona, where Tony opened several furniture stores."

"Yes, Mama told me, and I've written to her about my studies. Lucille sends me the best cards."

"Julia," Auntie resumed, "owns a beauty salon. Victor (her husband) finished a master's degree and is teaching at the Junior College."

Both women were my first cousins, twenty years my senior, and like sisters.

Auntie asks about my first year away from home and my classes.

"I never got homesick for Galveston, if that's what you want to know," I said.

My brother John worked a full-time job after school. "At home, I spent much time alone because Mama and John were always working. "At the dorm, I'm surrounded by people."

"Nice girls, I'm sure," Auntie looked to me for assurance.

I smiled and nodded, "All the ones in my dorm are former Catholic school girls, like me."

After a couple of hours on the road, Auntie stopped at the easement and opened the top.

Auntie had wrapped her long hair into a tight bun; mine was a curly pixy cut. The breeze felt as if fingers were rearranging my curls. The bright day gave vibrancy to a scene that consisted of acres and acres of flat landscape. In the distance, we'd catch a glimpse of an occasional isolated house surrounded by trees—a tractor parked in the drive. "That farmer must be home for dinner," Auntie would remark.

"I didn't spoil your summer plans, did I?" Auntie asked.

"Are you kidding!" I responded. "Galveston hasn't much to offer except a part-time job at Dairy Queen, summer school, or both."

She looked at me and opened her mouth to say something, but I quickly thought of a question so she wouldn't ask any more about Galveston. I deeply resented how hard Mama had to work after Daddy died. She'd completed a high school diploma, and a Practical Nurse's certificate yet could only find work as a maid with miserable pay at the home of a rich Anglo woman whose children disrespected her. I felt as if the Island had nothing to offer.

I asked, "Why do you want to find your baptismal certificate?"

"Baptismal certificates, at least those from Catholic churches, usually include family information. I want to see if my father's and grandparents' names are on it." She hesitated, then continued. "I want to see my father's signature."

I knew this story well about sixteen-year-old Lucia, Auntie's mother, and the Irish physician who ran away to a love nest in Tampico, Mexico. The lovers were together for three years, and Auntie was their firstborn. When Lucia was three months pregnant with a second child, shooters murdered the doctor. Without support, Lucia had to return home to Runge, Texas.

"It'll be nice to know some real family history, won't it," she laughed her distinctive chortle.

"How was your last day of school?" she inquired.

"Well, um, I'm only one of five Biology majors, and we each had to dissect our own preserved animals."

Auntie scrunched her face and asked. "How was that?"

"I hated it! We had to memorize the parts of the organs, the bones, and the system that circulates blood. We each got a huge frog, a Babel fish, and a big cat for the year. It ended up being more of an independent study, and I completed my assignments well before they were due because I wanted to get out of that smelly room."

"I would've, too," Auntie laughed. "Was it hard? You never had any trouble with school."

"No," I thought for a second, "I guess the hardest part was learning discipline."

"I don't believe that," she teased, "Tila was strict with you, and what kind of discipline do you need at an all-girls school?" She looked at me and raised her brows. "After all, they probably have more rules than your Mama."

"You'd be surprised," I retorted. "I had more freedom on campus than I ever had at home. We were allowed to come and go as long as we were in by curfew.

"And what was curfew?"

"Much better than home," I grinned. "Eight o'clock Sunday through Thursday, midnight on Fridays, and one A.M. on Saturdays."

"I can't believe it!" she said, opening her eyes wide.

I smiled and nodded. "At home, I was alone most of the time because Mama and John returned from work well after I went to bed. Many nights Mama worked all night as a companion for a sick person but would call to make sure I was fine. I'd place the phone in my bedroom, lock the door, and I could answer the phone without getting out of bed when she'd call to check up on me."

"Good thing for long cords," Auntie interjected, and we laughed.

"So now I'm completely on my own, surrounded by girls like me, and only a couple have boyfriends. We congregate in one room to chat; before long, someone engrosses us in her drama. We look at the clock; it's now after midnight, and that paper due tomorrow becomes a nightmare as I hustle to complete it."

"I love that," she laughed heartily, "Did you have any exams today?"

"No, I finished on Thursday, but, you know, a girl's school curriculum includes practicing Emily Posts' Book of Etiquette."

She looked at me questioningly, "What's that?" Just then, a semi-truck swooshes past us in the opposite direction, and the driver honks his horn.

"It's my car," Auntie responded, honking the horn to acknowledge.

I began to talk in an exaggerated proper tone like I'm Emily Post. "Make your bed and clean up after yourself. Wipe up any residue and water around the basin. Place soiled items in a laundry container.

Remember to always leave the work area clean and orderly for the next person."

"Do you think that boys' schools prescribe to that message?" I extended my index finger to my chin and glanced upward.

"NO!" we said together, laughing.

I looked out the window and saw a beautiful brown horse, his coat shimmering in the sunlight, running close to the fence that restrained him. He stopped, shook his head up and down, turned, and ran in the opposite direction.

"Look, Auntie," I pointed to the horse, "he's playing by himself."

"He's acknowledging my car," Auntie said mischievously and honked.

I continued to talk about student resident living. "I don't know anything about dorm life for a boy, but our dorm mother checked rooms weekly to ensure we made our beds, dusted the furniture, and stored personal items."

Auntie raised her eyebrows and seemed surprised.

"Once, during a lunch break, I forgot to pick up a teaspoon to stir my tea, so I stirred it with my knife. I never saw Sister Roseanna, the cafeteria proctor, but she tapped me on my shoulder and told me to get a teaspoon. I complained that I only had thirty minutes for lunch before my next class, but she wouldn't hear of it. I had to get up and get a teaspoon for an already stirred glass of tea."

Auntie then changed the subject. "Any lovers?"

That was classic Auntie talk in any setting, social or private. She wanted the chapter and verse, don't leave anything out of the story!

"No! As a freshman, the other dorm residents and I didn't date. Most were like me, from small towns and all-girls Catholic schools."

"Surely, with three military bases and several universities, you met some young fellas!"

She was determined to hear about my love life.

"Don't worry," I said, "even the nuns kept an eye on those of us who didn't seem to have a social life. I can't tell you anything juicy, but when our house mother thought some of us spent too many Saturdays on campus, she got us dates."

"Whaat?" Her incredulous look made me laugh.

"We'd gather in the student lounge to watch TV, talk, or play games. Sister would come in and say that three—or however many of us gathered—gentlemen were downstairs to escort us to Earl Ables, the diner across the street."

"So, Sister had an inside line to the barracks," she howled. "How did she do it?"

"I have no idea," I shook my head back and forth. "Ever had love at first sight?"

"No, not enough time!" I took a deep breath and lowered my tone. "I dated a true gentleman named Paul, who talked about his orders to Vietnam and what was going on there. I felt that he must have been scared. But after he left, I never heard from him again." I paused for a moment, then repeated, "I never heard from him again.

Maybe I didn't want to know."

We both were quiet; I hesitated a bit longer, then began discussing the other social activities.

"Every Friday, the Air Force or the Army dispatched a bus to take the girls to the base dance. It was so popular that only those with boyfriends stayed behind."

"I'm so impressed," Auntie said huskily with widened eyes.

"There was a DJ who played our favorite dancing songs like Wild Thing, R e s p e c t, Hanky Panky, all the popular songs," I shook my shoulders and sang My baby loves the hanky panky, ba pam, pam, pam…My baby…" Always ready to play along, Auntie snaps her fingers and repeats ba pam, pam, pam…

"I'd dance almost every dance. These dances didn't compare to the ones I went to in high school when the only time I got a dance was during the D. J.'s one lady's choice. I'd ask someone to dance, and I'd cringe while he'd take his time accepting. At the military club, the DJ would begin with the lady's choice dance, so I'd have a dance partner for the night if I wanted it that way."

"You didn't have a boyfriend in Galveston?" She looked at me like that was a big surprise.

"No! There was something about me that never attracted the boys in Galveston. I thought it was because of my orthopedic shoes and the limp, but it could have been the acne I got at puberty."

"Oh, that. Tila had acne when Mama brought the brood to Manhattan. I took her to the doctor. Your mother did the same for you, right?"

Auntie and Uncle Diaz had lived in New York, where they owned a Brownstone in Greenwich Village. During the Depression, Grandmother Lucia had taken her youngest three children to live with Auntie, hoping they would have a better chance of success.

"I got treatment at the doctor's," I said, "but I was always very self-conscious."

"Did you go to the prom alone?" She nodded and I felt that she understood. She had paid for my gown for the senior prom.

Kirwin was the all-boys Catholic school my brother John had attended.

"No, my friend Francine asked her cousin, a cadet, to escort me. I asked a boy from Kirwin, but he said no."

"And…come on, come on," she impatiently waved her arm.

"He had an excuse. I had asked John to tell him I was going to call to ask him to the prom."

"What was the excuse?" Auntie wanted to know. "He told me how flattering it was that I had asked him, then he told me no for that particular day. He finished the conversation by thanking me. It was very embarrassing."

"Was he Anglo or Mexican?" she asked.

While in college I was told by my dorm friends that I was too white to be Mexican. However, the girls from the wealthy families of Mexico who lived in the elite dorm with their maids considered the Mexican girls of Texas too ethnic and wouldn't even acknowledge our presence if we tried to speak with them. In Galveston, the undertones were barely perceptible, or maybe I was too naïve to pick up on the subtleties. After a year in San Antonio, I'd discovered the nuances of racism.

"Anglo," I replied after a long pause, "that part didn't occur to me until later. I just thought he would be embarrassed to be seen with me because of my feet and acne scars."

"So, nothing has changed in Galveston. That's the reason I moved around so much. I wouldn't say I liked the small-mindedness of some people in Texas City and Alta Loma. Mexican people can be just as prejudiced," Auntie said.

"I'd never thought about it," I responded. "It never occurred to me that I was never invited in the first place. Because Daddy and Mama were so strict, I couldn't spend nights at friends' houses or go on field trips."

"Ah, Querida," Auntie shook her head and gazed at me mournfully, "Those college dances give me hope that you will not end up a nun; I hope, I hope."

We both laughed.

"Your friend, Mrs. Salinas from Hitchcock, called Mama about her son wanting to ask me to his senior prom."

"Fina's son, el morenito, Jesse?"

"Yes," I smiled. Among Mexicans, one is either white or, moreno, brown skinned.

"And… come on," she gestured with her hand.

"I thought about how humiliating it felt when turned down for my prom, and I didn't want him to feel like that. I said yes."

Auntie smiled indulgently. "You made Fina very happy, I'm sure."

"Mrs. Salinas later mailed a picture of Jesse and me at the prom, and, I must say, we made an attractive couple."

Auntie smiled.

"She signed the back of the picture with Love you." Auntie didn't say anything.

"That was our only date."

We passed a sign; San Perlita 52 miles.

"Let's stop there," she pointed to the sign. "San Perlita and the surrounding towns and hamlets once belonged to our cousin. The Agostadero de San Juan de Carricitos land grant awarded by the King of Spain to Narciso Cavazos."

Auntie opened the center console, pulled out a map then handed it to me.

"It is now Willacy County. It was the largest territory ever awarded in South Texas—600,000 acres!"

"Let's get some dancing music going, please!"

I fumbled with the map as Auntie began working the radio.

Auntie was good at alternating subjects. She pushed the buttons on the radio and each station she picked was Mexican music. I didn't doubt that this trip would include at least one night of dancing.

"We're in Tejano country," I reminded her.

"Find us a station with lively Polkas and Cumbias," she instructed.

I didn't tell Auntie that I rarely listened to Tejano music, but I could list some songs I enjoyed.

A male voice came through the speakers singing a mournful ballad about everlasting love. I turned up the volume and sang along.

Auntie looked at me her mouth curled like she tasted something sour, "You like that depressing song?"

"Well, yes. Don't you think the words are sweet?"

"Can't you find something joyful and happy?" she answered.

She had a point and I scrolled through the radio stations looking for something more upbeat. After a bit of searching, I finally found a station playing Ranchero music, which was more upbeat but way too much oom-pah for me.

"That's more like it," Auntie laughed and moved her shoulders to the rhythm. I wasn't going to complain; I was so happy with this arrangement.

I opened the map, looked at the alphabetical listing of counties, and found Willacy.

"Auntie, I want to hear more about this land grant."

"It was family-owned for over a hundred years, with a few Cavazos still living on it today. Family members, compadres, and even Indians lived and worked the plots of land that Narciso gave them."

She turned to me and nodded, "Yes, we had Indians and even marriages between us."

I tried to recollect Mama's stories about marrying outside one's culture. Mixed marriages were faux pas. When my grandmother ran off with an

Irishman in 1897, she broke with the social conventions of her time.

"Later, King of the King Ranch and his partner, Kenedy, you know the King Ranch, "she turned to observe my acknowledgment, "won a suit against the Cavazos' heirs. They had the means and the political backing to get the land." She sighed heavily, "That was the beginning of the end."

"All I ever heard is that both King and Kenedy did a lot of shenanigans that eventually got them the Cavazos property," I said.

"That's right. First, the partners encroached on the Cavazos' land by fencing more than what was legally theirs. The settlers had an expression, 'Con el alambre viene el hambre.'"

"What a puzzling phrase," I uttered. "Wire brings hunger. What does that mean?"

"In those days, the land wasn't fenced. The branded livestock grazed freely, and the neighboring settlers' cattle foraged together. Cavazos cattle born on the range frequently weren't branded until a couple of years later, making them easy pickings. Indians weren't the only ones who stole unbranded cattle."

"Okay, so why did fencing cause hunger?" I still didn't get why fencing one's property was so devastating.

"Because encroaching on another's land narrowed the feeding area for the livestock, and the cattle began dwindling. Those enclosing the land could also barricade a few extra cows onto their property by fencing them."

"So, they were thieves, too?" Auntie nodded yes.

Just past a silo, we saw a gas station with a store. We stopped for sodas and gas. Oak trees canopied the countryside, providing shade and tranquility amongst the modest homes with large tracts of fenced-in land. I saw a field of corn beyond the gas station, ears standing crisp against the setting sun. The cluster of woods reminded me of the secluded trees on campus under which I studied and memorized the parts of the body for Biology class.

As the soft breeze delicately swept across my face and tousled my hair, Auntie pushed a button to close the top.

"It's getting dark. I don't want a Cabrón to climb in at a stop."

"I wonder what people do in a remote area like this," I mused aloud. "I like the bustling noises of San Antonio."

"Are you becoming a city girl?" Auntie smiled and edged toward the highway.

I thought sadly about how I neglected to listen to Mama when she told us stories about our family history. This time, I wasn't going to ignore Auntie's—she sparked my curiosity.

"How did Narciso acquire half a million acres of land?" "Well," Auntie responded, "Let me think about how to start?"

Chapter 2

THE TRAIL DRIVE

"Our family is part of the founding people of Texas, you know that, don't you? Auntie asked. I nodded. We had a long excursion to the Mexican border, and I wanted to hear about this unknown relative named José Narciso Cavazos. I didn't want to distract myself from the moment with talk about our recent membership into the historical society's First Families of Bexar County.

"Tell me about Narciso, Auntie; I want to know how we became the first Texans."

Auntie began, "You know, because of Hollywood, people think that the great cattle drives you saw on the TV started in Texas.

"Oh," I said, "Daddy loved to watch Rawhide." I referred to the television program with the handsome actor Clint Eastwood.

Auntie nodded. "These cattle drives began while Texas was still part of Mexico, long before the American Civil War. Ranching operations in Mexico had exploded with cattle kingdoms.

"I remember when Daddy took us to La Hacienda De Los Cavazos, and they seemed to have an explosion of sheep." I didn't mention how the animals stood to reach the high branches of trees and terrified my seven-year-old self. When they stood on their hind legs, they looked like monsters with massive horns that curved backward and pointed faces with chin beards.

"Yes," Auntie replied, "Sheep and cattle were the mainstays of the haciendas. Maybe I'll start with the trail drive, okay? The new settlement of Brownsville was 190 miles south of San Antonio and a popular spot for the trail drivers to rest. Understand this is around 1781, Narciso was waiting to hear a ruling that awarded him the land that eventually became the city of Brownsville."

★

The team, including Narciso's ten-year-old son, Manuel, the trail boss, Raúl, and a crew of five vaqueros, had completed a month-long cattle drive. Narciso whistled loudly, exhilarated over the safe delivery and sale of his family's cattle in San Antonio. He sat on his horse, Haro, and playfully coaxed him to rear. Narciso yelled a "whoop" as Haro galloped at high speed towards a thicket at the edge of the Rio Grande River.

The vaqueros were a team of faithful workers to the renowned rancher, Don Nazario, Narciso's grandfather. They were contractors, experienced in cattle drives, who went from one to the other.

Ramón, the cocinero, was highly energetic and always provided delicious meals, even when the provisions ended. He'd improvise by disappearing into the thicket to shoot a rabbit, a possum, or a rattlesnake. Ignacio, known as el Amante, the lover, composed songs about lost love, although married for fifteen years to his sweetheart when still in their teens. Francisco nicknamed el Lobo, still a bachelor at thirty-five, possessed a solitary lifestyle. He always carried a book and would sit under a tree to read, away from the group. At fifty, Vicente, called el Viejo, was the oldest vaquero. His body revealed a mass of iron muscles, and much younger men couldn't sustain Vicente's skill and stamina when rounding cattle during a stampede. Pedro, the youngest vaquero, began training as a thirteen-year-old after his parents were killed during an Indian conflict six years before. However, this team of vaqueros favored Don Nazario Cavazos, and they'd arranged their schedules whenever the Don needed cattle moved.

Don's grandson, Narciso, seemed to live fully engaged as a jack-of-all-trades. He did more physical labor than the other children of high-society haciendas. He not only accompanied the vaqueros on cattle drives, but he also brought his son, Manuel, on this one. Narciso stood at five feet ten inches but appeared taller due to his thin, solidly built physique. His ruggedly handsome face was never without a smile. Highly energetic and with a welcoming demeanor, he befriended everyone he encountered.

"I was born at Vallé del Pilón, founded as El Real de Santiago de las Sabinas in 1692 by Luis de Carvajal," Narciso informed the young vaqueros coming of age on his grandfather's ranch.

Raúl, his best friend and compadré, would first send Narciso the vaqueros seeking business with la Hacienda's Don but who were reluctant to approach him. "When Narciso appears in deep concentration and lost in thoughts, don't think he's being uppity. He's a vaquero; when there's manual labor, he's first in line hauling, joking, and sweating like a hired hand."

The ride home was swifter without a thousand head of cattle. Narciso yelled to Raúl, "Don't you think it's time to halt the caravan?"

Raúl smiled and hollered back with his usual affection toward his old friend. "Compadre, I figured long before you that you'd want to stop here.

After twelve hours since San Antonio, the group had another twelve for home. Narciso stopped at an old Indian crossing, a normal breakpoint near the Rio Grande, threw his bedroll toward the trunk of a massive oak, and dismounted Haro. The tree stood majestic among a grove of mesquite and pecan. A rocky stream gurgled nearby—the remote area was rugged with scattered large limestone rocks.

With his eyes sparkling with mischief, Narciso looked up at his son and said, "Manuel, keep alert to the wilderness and develop a keen observation for where you stop a trail drive. You never know what might hide behind the trunk of a large tree."

Manuel muttered and glanced around warily.

The trail master Raúl and Narciso had been born on the same day in 1750. Their mothers had grown up together, bonding the relationship between their sons. Their mothers claimed that their friendship had begun in the cradle. The boys were brought up as brothers and friends; they'd die for each other if necessary. Raúl was six feet two inches tall. His Spanish features of jet-black hair, white skin when he wasn't sunburned, and blue eyes refuted his mestizo origin. His ancestor, a Spanish conquistador, had won the hand of a Tlaxcaltec princess. The family possessed inherited land in Nuevo Leon, which his brothers and sisters maintained. Raúl was single, or so the community believed, and held a guarded and hidden intimate life. Only Narciso knew his secrets.

"Let's stay here by this grand oak," Narciso decided, and Raúl informed the vaqueros to set up camp. They were on the outskirts of Rancho Viejo near the colony of Brownsville, Tejas. Eleven years had passed since Narciso laid claim to the land in 1770, but the settlement was currently in a court dispute with Narciso and the occupants of the land.

"I want to talk, Manuel, about my dream for our future. I've never lost the lure for land here in Tejas." He turned to face Manuel, "Look at this land that I'm fighting for."

Manuel looked down from his horse Hondo, a blue roan Mustang bred on his great-grandfather's Hacienda. His eyes scanned the desolate landscape. He slowly dismounted and stepped onto the bushy grass that covered his knees. "Tallgrass, bushes, rocks, and trees," he responded. Manuel was as tall as his father and also slightly built.

"Manuel," Narciso rubbed the back of his neck, "your eyes and mind must constantly work to design a bigger future in Tejas with more land than you can imagine."

"You mean to build something from this nothing?" Manuel waved his arm in a semi-circle.

"We're halfway home directly across the River. We passed this very spot on our way to San Antonio; the cattle came right through here," Narciso swept his arm in an arc and turned around. Manuel blinked, turned his torso in a slow circle, stopped, and looked at his father. He said nothing.

"Where would you graze cattle if this was your land?" Narciso coaxed.

Manuel faced his father, who had given him this exercise on previous trail rides. "You mean when this is ours?"

"Yes," Narciso answered, "The court hasn't yet decided, but it will be soon."

Raúl jumped from his stallion Tlaxcala, a piebald-colored Mustang also sired at the hacienda. He roared with laughter. "That suit has taken eleven years. You still have that insane idea in your head, Compadre. You know this part of Tejas is unoccupied for a good reason; it's wild and dangerous. How is Maria Ignacia holding up? The lawsuit has to take a toll on her."

Manuel looked to his father, "What lawsuit? What does Mamá have to do with it?

The lawsuit began with Narciso and the De La Garzas, Don José, and Doña Maria Gertrudis, over a colony in Tejas the couple stayed on to develop around 1770, called Rancho Viejo. They and Narciso simultaneously laid claim to this land, and now both parties had petitioned the court for a decision on the rightful owner. Narciso didn't want to go into the details; his wife, Maria Ignacia, suffered much anguish over the dispute, which affected her physically. She was prone to headaches that developed after the birth of their last daughter, Ignacia. Over the years, the headaches escalated and confined Maria Ignacia for hours, sometimes days, to bed in a darkened room. The de la Garzas were her cousins, and, beginning in childhood, she had been close to the Doña. She had expressed to Narciso that the decade-long dispute "Leaves me with much anxiety, and these headaches feel as if my head will burst."

But Narciso continued to submit appeals—to Monterrey, then directly to Spain. As a descendant of conquistadors, Narciso wanted a name for himself. Texas was his opportunity to possess the land. In Spain, the aristocratic minority controlled vast tracts of land which granted not only privilege and prestige, but also power and influence.

"Your Mamá doesn't understand the big picture," he said to Manuel. "She's a woman and can't accept that I need to break out alone, without Grandfather's wealth. Turning to Raúl, he squinted his eyes and hissed, "You're always on her side, aren't you." Narciso knew that his beautiful and elegant wife enchanted Raúl.

Raul shook his head and grinned.

The vaqueros selected their spots and unpacked their sleeping bags. Ramón moved the chuck wagon to a clearing and began a fire. Ignacio strummed a guitar and sang a popular ballad. El Lobo joined in the singing—it was too dark to read. El Viejo went to the stream and removed his clothes to bathe. Pedro threw himself on the ground and covered his face with his sombrero.

Soon everyone sang while waiting for the sound of the triangle dinner bell. Pedro, still a teenager and the youngest, was ready to sleep. He lay down with his sombrero over his face.

Narciso closed his eyes and leaned against the giant oak. He listened to the voices singing and began to wind down in the tranquil setting.

Raúl removed Hondo's and Tlaxcala's tack and went over to Haro. The grey Andalusian had grown into a majestic, strongly built, elegant, ornery horse that only Narciso could control. Haro came as a yearling from the Iberian Peninsula, the Cavazos' homeland. Don Nazario presented him as a gift to Narciso on his twenty-first birthday. As Raúl reached for him, Haro reared and scooted away quickly to wander into the brushes, a habit he developed while still a colt.

"Don't worry; you devil, go ahead and ramble. Don't get stolen by an Indio," Raúl mumbled to himself.

"Sit here next to me." Narciso patted a bare spot near the tree and waited for Manuel to settle. "This is the story about your Abuelo, my Papá, José when he was 15. He accompanied his Papá, my Abuelo Don Nazario, on an expedition with its leader, Don José de Escandón. Their journey was a colonizing expedition into the Rio Grande Valley, this Tejas," Narciso extended his arm in a semi- circle. He looked at Manuel, who nodded, indicating that he was listening. "The Cavazos were part of seven hundred men that anticipated building settlements in this no man's land." With shining eyes, he looked at Raúl. Raúl grinned and stretched onto the ground covering his face with his sombrero.

"That was thirty years ago." Narciso shifted his weight and placed his hands on Manuel's shoulders. "My Papá planted that dream when I was around your age. When Papá died, I was twelve, and Abuelo Nazario believed I'd forget about my Papá's dream."

Narciso leaned back against the tree and closed his eyes. Such painful memories. One day, his father was robust and in high spirits; the next day, he had a fever and, in three days, died. Haro returned from his gander and snorted a fine mist on Narciso's face as he nuzzled him. Narciso laughed, "Haro, I'm fine." He stroked his satiny head. Just then, the dinner bell rang. Raúl jumped to his feet and slapped his sombrero against his leg. "Let's eat!"

The men were in a celebratory mood. They joked, told stories about previous drives, and devoured their meal consisting of a stack of corn tortillas, pinto beans, arroz con pollo, a salsa with diced tomatoes mixed with onion, garlic, chili Pequin peppers, avocados, and the juice of a whole lemon. Satiated, the men laid back close to the fire, tired and content. Vicente began recounting a tale, and everyone became alert. Vicente knew how to enthrall the men with stories of the early seventeenth century.

"We're on hallowed ground," Vicente began ominously. "We sit on the land of Indios that walked this very spot in a time before the Españoles," he pounded his empty canteen, startling Manuel. The men, used to Vicente's antics, laughed. "The Coahuiltecans are still with us and live among us. All of us have Coahuiltecan blood." Vicente looked for questioning looks among the men. "The Españoles came not only to indoctrinate the Indios but to pillage the land of her riches," he paused, then continued. "A band of young braves is probably watching us, waiting for us to sleep…" He leaped to his feet, and the listeners jumped, as if preparing for a fight.

Narciso and Raúl looked at one another and laughed. Narciso whispered, "These cold nights on the trail bring out superstitious beliefs, don't they?

The temperature dropped, and the night's blackness surrounded the camp. The men moved closer to the roaring campfire, blazing and sputtering, filling the air with smoke. Vicente kicked a blackened ember from the flames, which broke and crackled tiny sparks then began to smolder in the night's humid coolness.

"Comanche and Apache roam stealthily on nights such as this." Vicente lowered his voice, and the men leaned forward, eyes bright in anticipation. "They harvest wild plants and small animals. They take a calf, or two, or three, in case you didn't notice. When there's nothing valuable to steal…." Vicente hesitates, then quickly adds, "they kidnap the young!" Some of the men fidgeted. Manuel sat frozen, biting his lip.

"Do you know why they prefer the isolation in this no-man's-land?" Vicente stood and moved slowly around the men; he'd stoop before each face to stare deep into their eyes.

"They hide because they're thieves," Ignacio shouted, breaking the tension, and everyone laughed.

The tribe that followed the Spaniards to Nuevo Leon settled peacefully with them. "They hide to plan the attack!" Vicente draped a serape over his shoulders. "Several Indian groups from the colonized parts of Mexico survive here." He moved slowly, picked up each foot, and stepped softly onto the ground. He pointed to Ramón and said, "the Coahuiltecan."

He turned to Raúl, "the Tlaxcaltecs." Raúl grinned. He was a descendant of the tribe that joined the conquistadors to fight the Aztecs, their powerful enemy. Raúl rose to tell his story. "The Spaniards rewarded our loyalty with land and titles of hidalgos, yes, a lower nobility, and in perpetuity. That allowed my ancestors to carry arms and ride saddled horses, privileges denied to Los Indios under colonial rule. Also, no Spaniard can ever confiscate the Tlaxcaltecs' property.

Raúl sat, and the men roared a cheer with waving hats, "El Hidalgo!"

Vicente walked around the campfire. He smiled with a tightly closed mouth anticipating the men's rising excitement. With a hoarse whisper, he continued, "They're here now, tonight, in this place to destroy the Españoles. El Español is here! Now!" He turned abruptly towards Narciso and squinted. "He might seek revenge in the darkness!" Manuel took deep, slow breaths; he'd never heard this story.

Narciso, too, breathed in deeply. He felt the vaquero's eyes waiting for his reaction. He couldn't deny the history of the large-scale ranchers who enslaved Indios to the presidios for free labor.

Although never spoken, he was sure his ancestors did too. Spaniards in the community professed that the Indios could never measure up to the exceptional and high-class Españoles. Many were renowned conquistadores who descended from the Royalty of Spain like him. He shook his head solemnly and spoke, "You, my family's faithful vaqueros are Coahuiltecan whose families long ago inhabited the area where my ancestors settled. It is because of their willingness to collaborate and help us thrive that La Hacienda de Los Cavazos has prospered to this day. You will always be part of my family."

The men reaffirmed their loyalty to Narciso by shouting, "Patrón." Then, each man extended a fist and, in unison, pounded it against his heart.

Vicente warmed his hands near the fire and picked up the blackened ball- shaped ember. Cooled, he tossed it back and forth from one hand to the other. "The Indio ancestors established the trail. They paved the way and marked the path we now use for cattle drives. Didn't you notice that we were always near the water? He looked around and observed that while intrigued, the men's yawns indicated that they were slowly yielding to sleep. It was a long day, and he must bring the story to a quick end. "One last thing!" he shouted, and the men sat up startled. He tossed the cooled ember back and forth, and, in a hushed tone, "In the stillness of the night, you might hear the sounds of wolves. Or are they the sounds of wolves? Maybe it's the Indio coming to take revenge for his and his ancestors' plight. Tonight, keep your chaps and boots close by. If in the morning they're gone, check for a piece of coal next to your bed." He set the now-cooled ember next to Pedro. "You'll know then that the Indio also took a piece of your soul."

★

Narciso battled branches from the oak tree. His arms were pinned at his side and bound by... what? The weight on his legs made it difficult to move. He slowly awakened to the smell of coffee and bacon.

Turning to his right, the large mass of Haro lay against his body, his head on Narciso's legs. To his left was his son, tightly wrapped in his bedding, almost on top of Narciso's bedroll. No wonder he couldn't move.

Raúl stood with a cup of steaming coffee and threw Haro's tack at Narciso. "Your horse hisses when I come near him." He squatted next to Manuel, "Better get up. Ramón will pack the kitchen as soon as he finishes patting out the tortillas." Manuel sat up and rubbed his eyes. Leaning against the tree, Raúl grinned at Narciso, "Did the Indios spook your horse and Manuel?" Narciso ignored him. "Time to get moving, son; we got lucky. The Indios didn't bother us."

"I wasn't scared of any Indios," Manuel muttered. "It was softer ground next to you."

★

The caravan traversed the Rio Grande, where they had previously crossed the cattle. They anticipated a home arrival in time for supper in twelve hours. Father and son rode close together.

"Three years ago, Manuel, I sent a request to the Spanish Governor in Mexico City for land in Tejas."

Manuel's eyes widened, "Papá, why didn't you tell me before? Does Mamá know?

Raúl smothered a laugh and pressed his spurs gently against Laxcala, who responded by galloping away.

Narciso rubbed the back of his neck, "She doesn't have much faith for a future in Tejas. A day with no letter convinces her that God's plan is for us to remain at La Hacienda. She hasn't even seen the land, yet she calls it a forsaken wild country."

"It is a forsaken wild country," Manuel responded. Born in the La Hacienda De Los Cavazos community, Manuel thrived in Nuevo Leon's inhabitants' beauty and rich history.

Narciso's insides quivered every time he thought about the enormous changes in life. "Manuel, it means moving the family, servants, vaqueros who want to stay with us, and the stock to a place both Spain and Mexico deem non-occupiable land."

"Papá, can we also stay in our house and go back and forth?"

Narciso laughed heartily, "You know that everything belongs to Abuelo Nazario? He studied Manuel's worried reaction.

"Well, yes," Manuel answered hesitatingly, "but it's our house to live in, right?"

"I'm certain the house will always be there if we need it," Narciso replied. "But it's Spanish custom that the eldest-born son, my uncle, inherits the property when Abuelo and Abuelita leave this earth for eternity. I want my land to leave to you."

"What do you have to do?" Manuel asked apprehensively, "Once it's official, and we know we must leave?"

Narciso and Manuel lagged way behind when Narciso spotted the caravan clustering at a watering hole. Freshwater sprinkled down the rock of the massive mountain range, Sierra de Tamaulipas, gathering into a pond where the horses drank. The men dismounted and filled their canteens. Some walked around while others lay on the tall grass with their sombreros over their faces.

"Time for the noon meal. A cook's job is never done!" Ramón jumped from his wagon and hastily assembled tortillas filled with a mixture of leftover food, muttering as he loaded as much filling as he could into each corn tortilla.

"Los Indios say that Moctezuma used the tortilla as a spoon." He placed one into each of the ready hands. "Of course, hot stones kept the beans and chili warm." No one complained that the food wasn't heated. He spooned a final scoop of the beans and meat mixture into the last tortilla. "Las Indias brought wrapped tortillas to their men who worked long hours in the fields." The men turned their gaze to Ramón, who knew that look—they wanted more. "I saved the last one for me," he told them, raising his hand around the tortilla, "I'm here to feed, not to fatten." He smiled, satisfied that he had wasted no food on this trip.

Manuel continued beside his father when they broke camp. "Papa, who told you that you could own the land?"

"Remember the story about the leader, José de Escandón? My father, your Abuelo, and Abuelo Nazario, my grandfather, were part of his expedition. Did you forget?"

Manuel nodded and replied, "No, it happened thirty years ago, and you never forgot Abuelo Josě's dream."

"That's right!" Narciso reached out and patted Manuel's shoulder. "King Fernando VI commissioned Escandón as a Knight of the Order of Santiago, a venerable and noble military order. This title gave him jurisdiction, and he began mapping and establishing settlements along the Rio Grande."

"Is El Rancho Viejo the land? Is that why there is a dispute?" Manuel asked Narciso.

"No," Narciso hesitated before speaking. "The petition is undecided; Don y Doña José de la Garza began a colony anyway. I took them to court because I claimed that land too."

Less than four hours from home, the team entered the state of Nuevo Leon, leaving behind the Sierra de Tamaulipas, a remote, semi- tropical mountain range with no nearby cities or towns.

"Tamaulipas is very isolated," Manuel expressed.

Narciso pointed toward the mountains, "The higher elevations have forests of oak and pine that make it ideal for farming if not for the steep ridges. Your tutor taught you about 1518, right? This was where the Coahuiltecans lived when the Españoles encountered them during the time of Hernán Cortés."

Manuel nods, "Cortés conquered the Aztecs!"

"Several tribes fought with Cortés," Narciso corrected. "Over the centuries, the Españoles intermingled with the Tlaxcaltecs and the Coahuiltecans, a roving tribe who moved from place to place and settled in Leon, now Nuevo Leon. Shortly after the Españoles began settling in Nuevo Leon, many Coahuiltecans became ill and died. It was a mystery. Their numbers dwindled, so they intermingled with the Españoles, fell in love, married, and began their own families."

Manuel interrupted, "They moved back and forth from Nuevo Leon to across the Rio Grande River."

"Your tutor taught you the history of Nuevo Leon?" Narciso was taken a back.

"Yes," Manuel replied and continued, "Nuevo Leon was founded by our ancestor, Luis de Carvajal, the first governor of Nuevo León. He rose to the highest positions and brought most of his family with him. It's because of him that the family succeeded."

Manuel looked at his father. "But he was destroyed by the Inquisition for being a practicing Jew."

"Sadly, yes," Narciso responded. "1492 was the same year Christopher Columbus began his explorations into the Americas. "The Jewish community in Spain ended with King Ferdinand and Queen Isabella. They forced the Jews to convert to the Catholic religion. It was either that or burn at the stake."

"But Carvajal was here, in the New World, and the Inquisition followed him?" Manuel was incredulous. "King Philip awarded Carvajal large territories in Mexico, Texas, and portions of New Mexico."

"Yes, Carvajal came less than ninety years later, in 1579, but the Inquisition in Spain continues today," Narciso explained.

Manuel shook his head. "Carvajal discovered and settled most of the territories he was awarded. He brought settlers from Spain and Portugal to this New World. I don't understand. Is that why we're practicing Catholics? Were we ever of the Jewish faith?"

"Remember El Cid, our ancestor?" Narciso asked Manuel, who nodded yes.

"A knight and warlord in medieval Spain, he fought with Muslim armies to conquer the Moors. Wars between Christians and non-Christians have always been complicated and savage. But back to Carvajal, he brought his settlers from Spain, many of Jewish descent. The Inquisition had tried some of them for practicing Judaism, their ancestors' faith. Carvajal rescued them, thinking they could escape the Inquisition's tyranny. But, Manuel, you mustn't worry. Our family has always been of the Catholic faith."

★

Two hours later, the group approached another watering hole and stopped again. Raúl guided Tlaxcala beside Haro and, in jest, asked Manuel, "Are you ready to sign up a vaquero?

Manuel pushed Hondo between both men, took off his sombrero, and slapped it against his leg, mimicking Raúl's habit. "¡Absolutamente!" he yelled.

Narciso and Raúl looked at each other; together, they exclaimed, "¡Vamos a ver! We'll see!"

Manuel trotted Hondo over to his father, seemingly anxious to continue their conversation. "Papá, can anybody just take the land, or does it have to be granted by the King?"

"Excellent question, Manuel. Around the 1750s, the Spanish and Mexican governments dispensed land grants liberally to anyone living in Mexico, hoping to prevent foreigners from planning an occupation of Tejas."

"But the French were already here?"

"Yes, the French," Narciso acknowledged. "Spain doesn't want to lose Tejas to France."

"What do you have to do for the land, Papá?"

Narciso sighed, "An official process that takes a long time. I had to apply to the Governor in Mexico City, and I'm not the only petitioner."

"Is the land that valuable, Papá?"

"Land is everything. Remember, Manuel, you never sell the land if it's a choice between land and stock!"

"Yes, Papá, the land is everything!"

Narciso saw the caravan approaching the edge of town near the neighbors' ranchos and haciendas. The sun was setting. He continued, "Others applied when the government suddenly decided on this wave of colonization after they ignored settling Tejas for years. When the Governor received my petition for approval, he placed his official stamp and forwarded it to the King of Spain."

"How did you know what to say in your petition?" Manuel asked.

"I told the family's story," Narciso replied. "I emphasized our families' lineage and sacrifices to the Crown. We were 'old settlers.' I stated that my ancestors established roots in 1595 when they accompanied Conquistador Juan de Oñate, our relative, who forded the Rio Grande at the crossing point of El Paso del Norte in 1598."

Manuel beamed over his family's history.

Narciso smiled and continued with the story. "Escandón founded the town of Mier in 1753 at the pass of the Rio Grande on the other side of Tejas. Two years later, he granted our uncle, Tío Tomás Sánchez, permission to develop what is now the town of Laredo."

This thriving Southwest Tejas settlement of Laredo gave energy to Narciso's dream of a town with perhaps the Cavazos' name.

"I will build a grand hacienda for our family, and the land will be your legacy."

"Do we get the land for free?" Manuel asked.

Narciso laughed, "Nothing is free. I must comply with the rules that have been around since the Romans."

Manuel stared at his father, mouth agape! "The rules haven't changed since then?"

Narciso laughed again. "The grantee can only legitimately claim the title by living and cultivating the land granted."

"I don't understand; what does that mean?" Manuel asked, perplexed. "What will you have to do?"

"Five years after obtaining the land, I must build a hacienda, the major house, a community building, a church, a central plaza, and depending upon the number of people and the amount of land—a blueprint for a town."

They entered the range where Don Nazario grazed his vast stock of cattle and where Narciso learned about livestock farming. Many ranch hands herd the animals: cattle, sheep, goats, donkeys, and horses.

"All the skills learned from working this ranch I'll apply to our new land," Narciso said to Manuel, "you already know a lot, but you lack training in the cattle drives."

It was now dusk, and the temperature had dropped. Father and son, anxious for home, quickened their pace. They would regale the family at the dinner table with tales about the trail ride.

At the hacienda's entrance, Narciso dismounted Haro and told Manuel, "You go ahead." He watched from a distance—the vaqueros from the caravan dismounted and walked the horses to the farm building where the apprenticed vaqueros tended their horses. Freed from this chore, the men could hasten to their families after over a month's absence.

Narciso and Haro sauntered toward the vast plantation. His entire life had been on this Hacienda. Leaving it would be daunting. "Haro, are you ready for adventure?" Haro snorted his reply. The night was cold, yet there was a scent of Spring in the air. "What a majestic night," Narciso whispered, mindful of the stillness and tranquility. A cottontail scurried into the darkness, and Haro snorted in alarm. Narciso patted him, "It's only a rabbit." He looked up to the midnight blue sky. The brilliant stars conserved the secrets of the cosmos, conjuring magic in their brilliance. "Night is when I feel closest to the land," Narciso whispered.

"Papá! Papá! Papá!" Manuel ran toward his father. Narciso noticed his son's face and immediately thought the worst. He ran to meet up with Manuel.

"Papá!" Narciso held his son's shoulder and looked at his face ablaze with color and excitement. "What's happened?" Narciso squeezed Manuel's shoulders as he inhaled deeply, catching his breath.

"Mamá!"

"Something's wrong with your Mamá?" A sense of dread took hold in the pit of his stomach. Maria Ignacia suffered from sick headaches that lasted several days. He loved this woman, the mother of his children, but more than that, the elegance and tranquility she brought into his life.

Manuel stopped panting and gasped, "Mamá says that a foot soldier delivered a letter to the main house a week ago, and Abuelo sent a servant to deliver it right away. It's waiting for you at the house," he exclaimed.

Narciso broke into a run with Manuel and Haro following. When they reached the house's entrance, he turned to Manuel. "Take Haro to the farm building."

"No way, Papá, Haro bites!"

Narciso sighed deeply, "We'll go together." He drew Haro into the building, pulled off his tack, placed him in a stall, and latched the door. Only after Narciso and Manuel left did a young vaquero enter to tend to him. Haro snorted loudly and stamped his foot.

Both Narciso and Manuel raced to the house. Maria Ignacia waited at the hall entrance holding two-year-old Ignacia. Their daughters, twelve- year-old Maria de Los Santos and eleven-year-old Francisca stood behind her. Narciso hugged his older daughters and stopped to look at Maria Ignacia's face, beautiful and serene. "Hola, mi Querida," he whispered as he embraced mother and child. Maria Ignacia held on tightly. She pulled away to place Ignacia close to her sisters. At first, they kissed softly, then passion became more intense, and Narciso swept her into his arms and carried her like a bride. Maria de los Santos and Francisca smile and giggle. Manuel swooped his little sister, Ignacia, into the air with a whoop and holler. Narciso carried Maria Ignacia onto a settee.

"Can't a man give his wife a kiss," he asked his family. "The letter," Manuel could not contain himself.

"What letter," Narciso teased while his insides churned in anticipation. He looked at his family and turned to his wife.

Maria Ignacia didn't say a word as she rose from the settee. She removed an item from her pocket, locked her gaze on Narciso, and handed him the letter.

Narciso looked down. Prominently displayed was the seal of the Governor of Mexico City. His hands shook when he broke it to open the letter.

"Read it! Read it! His children screamed in chorus.

"Ok, ok, settle down." Narciso waved his hand and took a deep breath. This can only mean that the Rancho Viejo suit is finally settled.

Chapter 3

FAMILY TIME

Auntie finished her story about the trail drive, and we remained quiet for the next thirty minutes. San Antonio was now four hours away.

Driving along the extensive Texas highway gave only a sporadic view of civilization. It was dusk, and the lights flickering in the distance were the only indication of human existence. I gazed out the window, attempting to envision life during Narciso's time. Was the landscape void of trees like it is now, or had it once been a thick forest? Although there were no visible mountains, rolling hills appeared on the horizon. Did Indians on horseback look down to the valley, contemplating a battle with the settlers over lost lands, or did they sit tall and proud to revere the beauty of the sunset?

Auntie broke the silence, "It takes twelve hours to drive to Tampico, Mexico. You know that's where I was born after my parents ran away to a love nest." She wiggled her eyebrows. "We'll stop soon since it's almost dusk. A motel and a place to eat shouldn't be too hard to find."

"How do people live out here," I murmured.

"Huh," Auntie uttered while my focus remained on the fleeting landscape. "Oh," she giggled, "I loved living in Alta Loma with my farm animals."

"I remember," fondly recalling visits with her and Uncle Diaz. "John and I loved playing outside and pretended that the property's oil pump was pouring barrels of oil. We had to defend with swords and sticks we swung around like Caballeros. Did you ever get oil?"

Auntie groaned, "Maybe you'll learn some current history while we're on the road." She hesitated, "Pretty soon, we need a stopping point."

Knowing of her nearest neighbor miles away, I coaxed her into talking about Alta Loma. Were you lonely or wished you could just run next door for a visit?"

On occasion, Mama would sit on the porch of our house or lean over the fence holding coffee klatches with the next-door neighbors on both sides.

"Nothing ever stopped me from doing what I wanted," Auntie laughed. "We had a retired farmer who'd come over and help Diaz out with the animals and me with the vegetable garden. What kind of things did you get to do in San Antonio that you can't do in Galveston?"

I gazed toward the road ahead, leaned back, and sighed deeply. I didn't want to say that Galveston was not a happy place. My only success there had been in academics. I didn't date, couldn't get a part-time job, and most of my school friends spent time away from the Island during the summer while I was home all day. San Antonio, however, San Antonio was different.

"It was wonderful!" It was difficult to tell Auntie that I was one of those people who mostly kept to herself.

"San Antonio has several private colleges and universities, and, not to mention, three military bases. The weekends gave even the shiest girls the opportunity for social recreation. There were dances, outdoor tours, and campus events, like plays and lectures."

Auntie smiled, "Lectures? How political! What were you interested in?"

"Not politics; I pledged with the Alpha Psi Omega fraternity to be involved with the drama club."

"A fraternity?"

I laughed, "It was co-ed."

Auntie giggled, "I'm impressed! Tell me more about this Omega fraternity."

"The members assigned me to a big sister who gave me chores to complete for every performance—mostly grunt work."

Auntie grinned widely, "Making coffee, moving furniture, ironing costumes, cleaning the toilet?"

I laughed, "Pretty much along those lines. My assignment for the final initiation was to make drapes for an upcoming production.

"Oh boy," Auntie commented, "what was that?" "A huge bolt of a weighty fabric."

Auntie howled! "For costumes?"

I laughed too. "No, I had to make drapes for three full-sized windows on the set."

"Impressive," Auntie commented. "And...?"

"I had the sewing machine Mama bought me for my eighth birthday and I learned to make some of my clothes. Catholic schools required everyone to wear uniforms, and I wasn't always as stylish as the girls who shopped at Eibands or Nathans." These were the upscale stores in downtown Galveston.

"You were that young when you began sewing? I remember Mama Lucia making my sister's dresses and coveralls for my brothers, but I never was much interested in learning." She snickered, "I hated the look-alike dresses made like a pillowcase with three holes and a wide ribbon sash across the middle. She giggled again, "But the boys had it worse; their coveralls were made from flour sacks with the company imprint all over."

I loved hearing these bits and pieces of my grandmother. She had died before John, and I were born.

"Tía Rosaria," my aunt on daddy's side, "was a remarkable seamstress. She made my dress for the Junior prom based on a display in front of Nathans."

"You have the sewing gene from both sides of the family," Auntie chirped happily.

"Maybe, but I'm not very adventurous. I took home economics during senior year. The class project was to make a tailored long-sleeved blouse with French seams and bound buttonholes. Mama didn't have the money to buy material, so Tía Rosaria gave her a heavy white textured chenille fabric. It was bulky, and I had to sew the seams close so they wouldn't bulge when I wore the shirt. The finished blouse was so classic that Mama splurged on rhinestone buttons. My teacher graded it an A+."

"You have talent," Auntie pointed out.

"That may be, but I lacked the confidence to make a Vogue pattern— the money I saved with patterns I used for fabric. I stuck with the easy ones like McCall's and Simplicity which had various versions of the same outfit."

"When you got the assignment to make the drapes, did you panic?" Auntie shot me a concerned look.

"No, I secretly smiled. I'd been sewing long enough to know that someone at the fabric store would know what I needed, and I was right. The saleswoman showed me what supplies would make them easy to make."

Auntie chuckled, "What were they?"

"Drapery Pleat Tape and Pleater Hooks."

Her questioning expression indicated she needed more information.

"It was so easy. After making all the hems, the instructions called for sewing the tape to the top. With that done, simply insert the hooks, and voila, you have a pleat."

Auntie smiled, and I could tell she was proud.

I closed my eyes and thought about how much fun I had living in the dorm. I didn't feel confined, like at home, and enjoyed more independence. I only had to account for my absence when leaving campus. I didn't have to go far because various shops lined Broadway Street in Alamo Heights—the bank, a beauty shop, shoes, and clothing stores.

Auntie broke my pondering, "Every town we pass and the counties we cross once belonged to Narciso."

We were quiet for a moment, then I said, "Did you know that Mama submitted paperwork to the San Antonio Historical Society for John and me?"

Auntie nodded, "As descendants of the First Families?"

"Yes, on Daddy's side, John had compiled the research and genealogy for a college project."

Auntie is especially fond of my brother. Her pet name for him is Juanito which always made me smile when she spoke it. "What's the story?"

"Around 1730, 400 families were transported from the Canary Islands to populate Cuba, Louisiana, and Texas."

"I've been to Cuba," Auntie interrupted, "I went for a week and stayed a month." We looked at each other. "That was long before the restrictions."

I started where I'd left off: "The fifteen families included four unmarried men that finally arrived in San Antonio. That Post started as a mission with civilian households, but since the early 1700s, it was mostly military."

"And the men joined the military, which made sense—because now, they had an occupation," Auntie added. "How does Chon enter into all of this?"

Daddy was Encarnacion Esquivel Inclán but was known as "Chon."

"The captain of the Presidio, Joseph Urrutia, lived there with his single daughter, Juana, and she married Ignacio Inclán, the first of my great-grandfathers.

"Ahh, those Inclán and Esquiveles," Auntie sighed. Recalling Daddy's kin from her travels with us to Mexico, she added, "Very handsome men."

I laughed. "The Historical Society validated the research. John and I are certified as the ninth generation. They sent a certificate."

Auntie nodded with a smile.

"And" I continue, "Ignacio (Inclán) was also awarded a land grant.

"Well," she said, "Your Dad's mother is an Esquivel, and she inherited La Hacienda de Los Cavazos in Nuevo Leon that is still in Chon's family."

"Narciso lived in Nuevo Leon, and he is yours and Mama's ancestor. How did Daddy's side of the family end up with the Hacienda De Los Cavazos?"

Auntie looked at me in amazement. "Because your parents are related, didn't you know?"

Dumbfounded, I exclaimed, "No!"

"There's an old saying in Spanish culture—la sangre se busca. It loosely means that families married their children within their circle." She looked at me and quickly added, "In the old days, no one was allowed to marry outside of his or her social order."

I will definitely ask Mama about this revelation.

Auntie reached over and gave my arm a playful pinch. "I want to see if the Catholic Church in Tampico maintains old baptismal records. The house and land where I grew up in Runge are what remained of the land grant, and the church records are probably all gone now. Only a few of the Cavazos could hold on to their ranches. But don't worry; you'll have at least a week or two to hear the stories."

"Mama and Daddy told John and me wild tales for bedtime stories," I reflected, "while fun to hear, we'd rather believe more in fairy tales."

"Tell me one of your mothers," Auntie said. "Hmm."

"Mama told stories about Captain Juan Cavazos del Campo and Don Juan Canales, two dashing noblemen from Spain who came to Mexico with the conquistadors."

"Yeess," she hissed, "the adventures of our ancestors."

"These stories were more like an Errol Flynn movie." I knew she would recognize the actor who played the swashbuckling role of Robin Hood that we saw at the theatre. "Mama would describe the rebel leader, General Antonio Canales, warring with the Indians who didn't want to give up their land." I turned to see her reaction. "He was a lawyer, by the way."

My grandfather, Auntie's stepfather, was a Canales, and I wanted Auntie to acknowledge our assertive and headstrong family members. Auntie didn't comment, so I continued.

"Mama gave a vivid description of the drama and the legend regarding Antonio—Apache wars in Mexico; his attempt to establish the Republic of the Rio Grande in Texas."

I laughed at the slow disbelieving shake of her head. "I know; what would our life have been like if Texas had become an independent country."

While nodding slowly, Auntie pointed out, "He wasn't killed nor sacked by the government, though."

"No, Antonio eventually abandoned the rebellion's attempt that lasted less than a year and received a commission as Brigadier General in the Mexican Army."

With her head cocked and shaking slowly, Auntie exclaimed, "To think Tila kept these ancestors alive with her stories. Good for her!"

Only then did it dawn on me that Mama's stories were our history. "And I only wanted to hear about Cinderella and Sleeping Beauty," I confessed.

"I remember when Mama Lucia told those stories," Auntie recollected,

"I'd sass her with comments like "…if we were so famous, where did all the money go?'"

I wondered if Granddad José inherited this spirit, this son of the devil, from his ancestor. I never knew my grandad. He was killed in the 1947 Texas City Disaster. Mama talked about him; she told me he traveled extensively as a railroad engineer and was home sporadically. He drank heavily at home, and he and my grandmother would have knockdown drag-out fights. My parent's conflicts were never violent, although both would raise their voices behind the closed door of their bedroom. However, I still did not understand the relationship between my grandfather and Auntie and kept my mouth shut.

"Tila loved her Dad very much," Auntie pointed out under her breath.

"She did," I replied, "often talking about him. She even told me about when she went to Mexico to get his papers to return to Texas."

"Your Mama was pregnant with her first child," Auntie pointed out, "it had taken almost ten years, and she wanted José to meet his grandchild."

We were silent for several minutes. That child would've been my oldest sibling. What might life have been like with two older brothers? My parents never talked about that baby.

"Getting back to Narciso," I chattered, "The land grant must have been very desirable."

Auntie looked at me and shrugged her shoulder, "In Narciso's will, he never wanted to sell the land. Maybe Juanito can do more research."

"Why weren't you baptized in Mexico?" I asked, returning to the reason for this trip.

"Don't know," she replied, "could have something to do with godparents, maybe? Since my parents were not from Tampico and were unmarried, there was nobody to pick."

I understood the importance of godparents because Mama said that they were the ones who would care for a child should the parents die.

Daddy was fifty when I was born, and Mama was thirty-seven. They chose as my godparents the teen son and daughter of their best friends, who agreed to my spiritual and physical upbringing if my parents died before I was of age. Instructed in Catholic schools since kindergarten, I never questioned any consequences that could arise from this guardianship arrangement. Mama had six living siblings, one of whom would've taken my brother and me in a flash.

"Maybe godparents were meant to ensure that their godchild practiced the Catholic religion," I remarked.

"I'm not deeply religious," she grinned, "God doesn't want me, and the devil doesn't either."

I heard this on more than one occasion, especially at funerals where the comment would bring laughter to the solemn congregants.

We both looked at the clock. "It's 5:30. Didn't I pick you up at one?"

We've been on the road for four and a half hours and two hours from Brownsville. I don't like driving after dark," Auntie divulged.

We saw the signpost that Port Isabel was 22 miles away. Thirty minutes later, Auntie turned into the Queen Isabel Inn, close to a business district. "This place looks lively, so we'll stop here. I prefer places that look busy."

We checked into a small room with one double bed, a tiny kitchenette, and a bathroom; we placed our suitcases in a wall carve-out with hangers that served as the closet. Auntie bounced up and down on the bed and nodded in satisfaction. "I'm hungry for shrimp."

To the right of the Inn, an arrow pointed to Pelican Station, a section with shops and restaurants. We walked to Pirate's Landing, just next to a long pier. The restaurant with the sign "fresh shrimp caught daily" attracted Auntie and we entered. The place had outside seating and we sat close to the railing near the water. We stepped outside—it felt great to move around—and I breathed in deeply the familiar salty air reminiscent of Galveston Island. The fragrant breeze was cool, and the stunning golden sunset, whose rays slowly announced the day's ending, had vanished entirely. The relaxing sound of water slapping against the pillars of the pier and the distant nostalgic caws of seagulls completed the tranquil setting.

Almost in a whisper, Auntie spoke.

"This reminds me of when your uncle Diaz and I had a home near the ocean in Long Island."

I didn't know about Long Island. "Didn't you live in Manhattan?"

"We had a bungalow, but I got restless. I thought I'd make a good apartment manager." She looked at me and laughed. Then her eyes dropped to her hands. "I learned that a Brownstone was for sale at a good price in Greenwich Village. We should never have left that bungalow; Jr. drowned in the Hudson a short distance from the Brownstone."

Auntie was referring to her first, Aurelio, my first cousin. He'd been born when she was eighteen. His was the second family tragedy for Auntie and Uncle Diaz. The story of his drowning appeared in the newspaper, and Mama had a clipping in a photograph book:

Rumors of a barrel murder were dispelled yesterday afternoon when the body of Aurelio Diaz, 8 years old, of 527 West 52nd street, was found in the North river at West 52nd street by Patrolman Beyers of the marine division after grappling for several hours. Early Friday night the youth's father went to the West 47th street police station and reported his boy missing. Detective Leach, who was assigned to investigate, was told by Herman Ludecke, a 7- year-old (sic), who lives in the same house as Diaz, that "two boys had put Diaz in a barrel, loaded him on a white wagon with a pickle painted on the side and drove off with him." The police started searching for the wagon, but when it was learned that children had seen young Diaz later in the evening, they abandon (sic) the kidnapping theory. When the body was recovered, William O'Keefe, 7 years old of 53 West 52nd Street, said that he had been playing with young Diaz on Friday evening when the boy fell off the pier at 52nd street.(sic) [i]

We were quiet during our meal. When we finished, Auntie took me by the arm, "Let's walk towards the Boardwalk."

She spoke softly, "I'm very impulsive—like wild hair gets up my ass."

She looked at me for a reaction, and I just smiled. I'd heard Auntie's colorful vocabulary before and didn't find it offensive.

"I'd sell a valuable property, then, down the road, fortune turned it around for the person that bought it. Remember I was going to tell you about the ranch in Alta Loma?"

I smiled, thinking about Auntie and Uncle Diaz's unusual relationship for the times. They were more like business partners, with Auntie being its top executive.

Auntie waited for me to respond. "Yes…yes, the one with the oil pump."

"We'd been married about ten years and had three furniture stores. Our baby, Roberto, died when he was two." She turned to me, "Do you know about him?"

I nodded that I had. Another first cousin in my family history, Roberto, had died in Galveston.

"A brain tumor, right?"

"Yes, and I wanted out of Texas. So, we moved to New York and bought the Brownstone, where we lived for fifteen years."

I was well aware of how parents carried the death of a child as their companions in grief. Auntie lost two young children, and three of her sisters lost youngsters as well. In the 1931 Depression year, Aunt Sophie's toddler died in New York of an unknown infection prompting the family to move back to Texas City, where, eleven years later, she lost a fourteen-year-old son, Bobby, in the Texas City Explosion. Also killed were their youngest brother, my uncle Alex, their father, my grandfather José, and a young nephew-in-law married to one of my favorite cousins. The body of Aunt Sophie's son was never found, and she wore her sorrow like a veil. Aunt Genevieve lost her one-year-old in 1946, which prompted her family to move back to Texas. They returned to New York following the Texas City Explosion—death and traumatic injuries rendered overwhelming heartbreak. My parents lost their firstborn on the delivery table—a stillborn. My aunts and uncles taught me more about the baby, as my parents rarely mentioned this lost infant.

"Mama told us much about living with you in New York," I told her. "I was too strict, I suppose," she murmured, and I laughed.

One of the advantages of my grandfather's position with the railroad, Grandmother had access to free tickets. She took her youngest three children to New York during the Depression, hoping they'd have better opportunities than in Texas City. Grandmother died 11 months later and was buried in New York City.

"Tila, Genevieve, and Alex were teenagers; of course, you had to be strict."

"But then," she began again, "everyone began leaving to return to Texas. I missed them. We sold the Brownstone and bought the ranch in Alta Loma."

"If you had stayed in New York, I'd probably never have gotten to know you and Uncle Diaz," I reminded her.

She looked at me in amazement, "You know what those Brownstones are selling for now!"

I shook my head no.

"Well, the property in Alta Loma had a pumpjack, and we heard there might be oil. We never checked because I wanted horses, cows, and chickens." She laughed, then sighed.

It was well-known that Auntie preferred animals to humans. Like when she stole a turkey off a pick-up truck during Thanksgiving week because she suspected it would be the holiday dinner. Whenever the vet came to the ranch to examine her animals, the turkey, which John, and I named Gobble, also received his physical exam.

"I remember staying at the ranch," I said fondly. "We'd run the chickens all around the field, and when we grew bored with the chickens, we'd chase the cows." "Yeah," Auntie commented, "y'all were rascals. The cows wouldn't give milk, and the chickens didn't lay eggs for a week after you guys left."

I hadn't known and laughed loudly. "You were going to tell me, was oil ever discovered?"

She reflected before responding, The real estate agent posted the sign for the house and land Diaz, and I were selling. We'd initially intended to keep the small parcel of land that had the pumpjack. But when the proposal came from the people buying the house, they offered a lot more money if I included that small parcel of land with the pumpjack. We were moving on again, and I wanted the money for the house we're in now." Auntie lived in California and had a home in Imperial Beach.

"And the new owners didn't waste any time consulting an engineer who did the magic to get the oil pumping again."

"When you and the other aunts tried to get Mama to move to California after Daddy died, we were young enough to make the change, but John didn't want to, so we stayed in Galveston," I remembered the fuss he made, and Mama didn't pursue it. The thought of multiple moves was foreign to me. "I lived in the same house all my life," I said.

I thought glumly about how hard it was after Daddy died and Mama worked so many low-paying jobs. She'd come home exhausted and would go immediately to bed. In the morning, she'd noticed I'd cleaned the house, hung out laundry, and cooked a meal. She'd comment on how grateful she was for the least of what I did to make her life easier. It could've been easier; I'd thought many times. Aunts Sophie and Genevieve had already moved close to Auntie in California. It would've been fun to have had the companionship of cousins my age instead of being alone in the house all day. My brother was in Houston, attending college and working full-time during the summer. I never had the freedom my classmates enjoyed. Even when Daddy was alive, my parents had the old-fashioned notion that a daughter needed a chaperone. Had my father lived, I probably would never have gone to college in San Antonio or worked. I had Dairy Queen as the only prospect for a job that previous summer. I could take the required Civic class at Galveston Junior College, a few blocks from my house, but that was all the summer offered—until Auntie's trip.

Auntie seemed to have read my mind and looped her arm into mine. "I met Diaz in Galveston at a dance," she turned and faced me, mischief in her eyes, "just like one of your dances when groups of young people gathered."

She was trying to change the mood, and I smiled gratefully at her perception.

We passed a souvenir shop with a mermaid in a seashell-shaped brassiere at the entrance. Auntie stopped, "Wanna go in?"

"Not really," I was more interested in Auntie's story. "We have shell shops in Galveston."

We continued to walk, and Auntie looped her arm in mine once again.

"I was sixteen living in Galveston with my godparents because of that Cabrón," Auntie's stepfather José, "and we went to a fundraising dance, you know, one of those affairs to take your mind off the hurricane's destruction." I was all too familiar with hurricane destruction.

We turned at the end of the pier to retrace our tracks. The boardwalk wasn't as crowded.

"Let's head back," Auntie said and continued, "Diaz was twenty-four when WWI broke out. His parents emigrated from Spain to Cuba to escape having their sons drafted, but Diaz departed to the United States and got drafted anyway," She laughed.

We passed restaurants still emitting the aroma of coastal cuisine.

"We met in 1915 after the hurricane in Galveston, and the Army sent troops for disaster relief. Whoever organized the dance invited the soldiers."

"Was it love at first sight?" I teased back, giving her a taste of her own medicine.

"Of course!" she answered quickly and bumped into my shoulder, "his blue eyes were irresistible."

We had a good laugh. I loved my Uncle Diaz; he was a gentle soul who loved the outdoors more than indoors, where everyone sat around the kitchen table gossiping about neighbors, talking about child- rearing, or sharing the latest family scandals.

"Remember when you brought Uncle Diaz to our home?" During the high school summer break after junior year, Auntie dropped Uncle Diaz off in Galveston. I hadn't seen him since they left Texas, and he rarely, if ever, traveled with Auntie. "He said you tricked him into coming. How did you do that?" I was curious because he stayed at our home, and we only saw Auntie when she dropped him off and picked him up on her return to California.

"Mama left me with the car because I was the only one who didn't work."

That summer, a week after completing my sophomore year in high school, I was scheduled for right-foot triple arthrodesis and a bilateral tendon lengthening. The orthopedic surgeon had written the procedure on a prescription paper that I kept in my wallet.

Because both my legs were in casts up to my hips, I lay in a hospital bed for two weeks in May, all of June and July, and two weeks in August. A couple of weeks before school began, I was discharged for physical therapy to build up the strength in my legs so I could walk. I'd lost a lot of weight during the surgery, and after two weeks of physical therapy, I'd lost even more. Mama fretted my entire junior year over the weight loss. She felt that I still hadn't completely recovered from the extensive bone surgery and preferred a restful summer over a part-time job. "That's why I was the only one home."

Auntie thought for a long minute, "I remember," she then burst out with laughter. "I said to Diaz, 'Let's go for a ride.' He was like a child and rushed to the car. He thought we were going to the beach." She giggled. "After a while, he knew it wasn't the beach. 'I need clothes,' was all he said." Auntie laughed harder. "I told him his suitcase was in the trunk. He sighed, and that was it."

"Poor Uncle Diaz," I felt terrible for him.

"For what? He had a great time. He told me he liked how you drove— faasst!"

I couldn't help but laugh. There wasn't much in Galveston to entertain Uncle Diaz, so he was my ride-along, and I always used the ocean boulevard for any destination so he could enjoy the beach.

★

I woke up early the following day, anticipating another five hours of travel. Auntie didn't stir, and I stepped into the bathroom, making as little noise as possible. When I finished, Auntie sat in bed with a map spread before her.

"Good morning," we said to each other.

"You know," she looked up, "we're only thirty-two miles from Brownsville and the border crossing. I haven't seen Tía Rita in years. After breakfast and sightseeing, let's make that a stop."

Tía Rita is my maternal great-aunt, and I was surprised she was still alive.

"I hadn't seen her since I was eight when Mama brought us to visit her and Aurora," her daughter and caregiver. "It's been eleven years, and she looked 100 years old then."

"Come look," she held her finger to a spot on the map.

"Beginning here at Robstown along the coast of Kenedy, Willacy, and Cameron counties and toward Matamoros…." She circled the area with her finger so I could see how vast the sections she pointed to were. "All this included the Land Grant."

"Wow!" I exhaled.

We had breakfast at a café. The proprietor took our order, and Auntie engaged him in conversation. He moved over to our table when the last customer left. "You're in for a real treat," he told us in a familiar Texan drawl. "Port Isabel has an intrigue with a lighthouse in the town square. There's a guide who will fill your head with haunting ghost stories and pirate tales. Legend has it that South Padre Island has an undiscovered treasure."

A part of the National Park Services, Padre Island on the coastal tip of Texas offers beautiful beaches and warm gulf waters. I remembered Narciso's son, Manuel, was engaged to Pilar Balli, the daughter of the original grantee of Padre Island.

"Have you gone in search of such treasures?" Auntie teased.

"No, well maybe, once," he laughed. "There's a scuba school in South Padre Island that takes adventurers out, and I tried it once. Then I determined that I preferred my feet on solid ground."

We thanked the proprietor and took our leave to explore.

Auntie wanted souvenirs, so we entered a shop just as it opened. When we returned outside, a man with "Guide" embroidered on his pocket flap passed out a flyer and motioned us to follow. When he amassed about ten people, he stopped and gestured to surround him.

"This is the site of Fort Polk," he began. "Mexican cattle ranchers developed a village here in the 1700s. Some ranches are still in existence today."

I whispered to Auntie, "I wonder if Narciso did business with this fort."

The guide continued, "Abandoned just before the Mexican American War of 1846, U.S. forces led by General Zachary Taylor occupied the point and established a depot to receive regiment supplies from New Orleans." He raised his hand toward a watchtower. "The lighthouse provided a beacon for the ships bringing guns, ammunition, and other wartime supplies to the soldiers stationed here with Taylor. It is well known that the Mexican ranchers provided the beef."

"Hmmm, could the Cavazos Ranch heirs have been the suppliers?" I wondered out loud to Auntie.

The guide drawled on, "The fort was abandoned in 1850, but the colony it attracted developed into Port Isabel. Many soldiers became enamored with the area and, after the war, returned to buy land and set roots."

"Yeah," Auntie whispered, "those cabrones stole the land." "Was that how Narciso lost his?" I whispered back.

He concluded his short presentation, "Come back at 2 P.M. to hear about the ghosts of the Rio Grande and its buried treasures." He maneuvered the crowd to a donation box. Auntie shoved a bill through the opening, and we walked the boardwalk.

"Port Isabel looks a lot like Galveston," Auntie observed. "You know that the debonair pirate, Jean Lafitte lived on both islands, right?"

I remembered reading about his colony of 1,000 people. "He burned the town when forced to leave," Auntie added. "I didn't know about the fire."

We came across a plaque:

Legend has it that in the early 1800s Jean Lafitte, privateer, and a smuggler who interrupted his illicit adventures to fight heroically for the United States in defense of New Orleans in the War of 1812, found refuge at Port Isabel, and formed trading alliances with the local ranchers, who appreciated the quality of his contraband.

"So, this is where he came when forced from Galveston, and the Mexican ranchers traded and bartered for his booty."

Auntie shrugged. "Maybe."

★

Our first stop in Brownsville was for freshly baked pan dulce, Mexican sweets, still warm from the oven. Aurora answered the door and embraced Auntie in a long hug. She then pulled me toward her and gave me a tight hug. Tears streamed down her face. Both women were quiet with emotion.

"How is your mother," she asked. "I still feel bad that I was unable to make it to your Dad's funeral." It had been seven years since his unexpected death, and I still felt pain when someone mentioned him.

"I understand—Mama's fine." Auntie held up the warm fragrant bag.

Tía Rita was in a wheelchair staring out the living room window. Auntie and I embraced and kissed her. She looked at us blandly; her soft wrinkled face displayed no sign of curiosity or recognition. She was nicely dressed, with her hair pulled back in a bun. Jewelry adorned her ears, neck, and wrist.

"Aurora, she looks wonderful," Auntie complimented.

A child around two happily screamed from a playpen and extended her arms for Aurora to pick her up; she placed her on the floor and handed her a baby bottle.

"What a beautiful baby," Auntie cooed.

"She's my grandniece, Corina. Her mother, Consuelo, attends junior college and works part-time. Since I'm home all day, I watch her. She's no trouble, and she and Nana entertain each other."

Aurora was around fifty, Mama's age. Although divorced for many years, she remained single with no children of her own.

Corina toddled over to Tía Rita, sucking on her bottle. In a flash, Tía snatched the bottle and began sucking. Corina screamed, "No!" "Mine!" Aurora jumped from her chair, retrieved the bottle, and returned it to Corina, who promptly returned it to her mouth.

I was startled and tried not to laugh, but I thought how horrified my mother would've been at returning this unsanitary bottle to a baby!

Aurora sat again and asked, "Why are you going to Mexico?"

"Just showing the girl our childhood haunts and giving her, what appears to be, a history lesson on the Cavazos,'" Auntie explained as Aurora prepared a tray with coffee.

Aurora stopped and gave me a long look. "Oh, my," her smile appeared frozen, but the expression quickly disappeared. "Are the skeletons coming out of the closet?" She took an uneven stride and hesitated before setting down the tray, her face a deep red; she looked at Auntie.

"Oh, come on," Auntie declared, "you think we're the only family with dark secrets, a real skeleton? Maybe not this trip, but the next one, I'll show her all the places Hijo del Diablo took us to live while Mama had a baby at each spot."

My eyes widened at Aurora's reaction and Auntie's revelation. I thought to myself; I'm going to learn a lot of juicy stuff about the family—a dark secret. I couldn't wait to find out.

★

After a couple of hours with Auntie and Aurora catching up with family goings-on, we rose to leave. The cousins held on to each other for a time. Neither Auntie nor I said a word. Aurora, with tears, stood watching us as we drove away until she became a speck on the outside mirror.

"I'm glad we visited," Auntie finally said.

"Me too," I responded.

★

Auntie and I prepared for the night and sat in bed, talking. "Want to hear more about Narciso?"

"Of course," I responded excitedly, "I can't wait."

Auntie looked at me, "Let me tell you about his first wife, Maria Ignacia."

Chapter 4

MARIA IGNACIA

"Just think, if the court had awarded Rancho Viejo to Narciso, we'd be the pioneer descendants of Brownsville, Texas, instead of the Don and Doña de la Garza," Auntie said. Of course, A man named Stillman, an Anglo, is credited for founding Brownsville." She then softly repeated the lost opportunities involving the Brownstone and the oil well. "Maybe I inherited that fortune belongs to others' genes from Narciso," I didn't respond.

"Aside from that," Auntie continued, "Maria Ignacia came with a pedigree. She was a Balli but also a Báez Benavides from her mother's side. Do you remember I told you that old families with ties to Spain didn't marry outside their class?" She waited for my answer.

"La sangre se busca," I repeated, and she nodded.

"Maria Ignacia descended from one of the founders of Monterrey. So, her marriage to Narciso, the ancestor to royals, must have been the wedding of the century in Nuevo Leon." She got up from bed and went to the bathroom for a glass of water, "She must have been the "belle of the ball" in her youth and first in line for the most eligible of men. She was five years older than Narciso. Who knows why she didn't marry in her teens as many women did then?

"Maybe her parents held off marriage proposals for the 'pick of the litter,'" I giggled.

"She'd be giving up a lot of comforts if the family moved to Texas," Auntie said. Think about how terrifying starting from scratch had to have felt after living the twenty-one years of marriage in the one place she loved."

★

In 1790, Tejas was a desolate place. Eleven years had passed since the eleven-year conflict had ended between Narciso and the De la Garzas—but not Narciso's nonsense about moving to Tejas. This unresolved matter of Tejas kept Maria Ignacia in an anxious state. Every day, she gathered her daughters to pray the rosary to La Virgen de Guadalupe, the patron of Mexico, reminding them to ask for her intercession that Narciso abandon his intentions to upend their life. Their older children were now of marriageable ages, and obtaining any eligible prospects was unlikely for her daughters in such a remote region. Her only consolation was their ongoing negotiations with Don and Doña Santiago Balli over their daughter Maria del Pilar's betrothal to Manuel. The Ballis owned many leagues of land called Padre Island and were wealthy.

That evening, Maria Ignacia bravely began the conversation, knowing that Narciso had something on his mind. "Narciso, I'm convinced the court awarded the Rancho Viejo because the De La Garzas began the now budding colony of Brownsville. They never left the land to live back in Nuevo Leon; they pressed on with developing their small community." She climbed into bed and adjusted the covers.

Narciso, still preoccupied, responded, "Querida, I'm not going to stop until I get an answer that lets me know once and for all that the King will never grant me any land." He, too, got into bed.

"With the children now older, we should be looking forward to weddings and grandchildren," she expressed to Narciso, whose deep, even breaths told her he was already asleep.

The following day at breakfast, Narciso informed Maria Ignacia, "I've submitted several requests to own porción of land in the undeveloped terrain of Tejas." He watched for his wife's reaction.

A servant girl brought to the table Maria Ignacia's breakfast; sliced apples, a hard-boiled egg, and a basket of still-hot biscuits.

"So," Maria Ignacia accused, "you put on a happy front around your vaqueros, but when alone with me, you continue to obsess over Rancho Viejo."

"I'm not obsessing over el Rancho," he offered quickly, "I intend to get something better."

The servant returned with Narciso's plate filled with huevos rancheros, his favorite egg, bean, and tortilla dish. He poured the freshly made Chile pequin salsa covering the entire plate. Maria Ignacia sat back to marvel at the spectacle. Narciso's face turned beet red, sweat and tears pouring down his face. She shook her head, fascinated at how this discomfort could be so enjoyable when even a simple diet couldn't bring her pleasure.

When they finished, she rose from the table and stepped into the house, Narciso directly behind her. He went to his favorite chair and sat with his head back, eyes closed. She gathered her crochet basket and sat on a settee facing him.

"I thought the De La Garzas would remain in Nuevo Leon until the suit settled. But instead, they risked everything when they moved to the land and expanded," Narciso admitted to Maria Ignacia. Land grantees usually lived in their primary homes while vaqueros, slaves, and Indios readied the occupation. "If that made the difference, we would have occupied that land a decade ago."

Maria Ignacia sat serenely crocheting lace for a christening gown. Emilia, her servant, had recently given birth, and Maria Ignacia would guide this young mother on her obligations for the baby's baptism ceremony.

"Isn't that one of the terms for a land grant, 'settling the land?'" She offered softly and looked at Narciso. "Don't you think the court awarded the land to them because they complied with the conditions outlined in Spanish law to settle permanently within five years?

Narciso didn't respond. He rose from his chair to pace back and forth. "I've had this dream for most of my life, and I've made many plans, and now…" "The stock I raised in preparation for Tejas will now have to be moved and I'll have to start all over with the stockbreeding." He turned to face Maria Ignacia.

"This land plan you greatly want, Narciso, is postponed, not over." Maria Ignacia winced as a sharp, stabbing pain pierced her temple. She tried to ignore the ache and breathed deeply.

The headaches began with their last baby, Ignacia, but she blamed these painful attacks on Narciso's fixation on Tejas.

"Besides," she continued, "we have a fulfilling life here near family and friends." She closed her eyes and leaned back. The dreadful throb that began at her left temple and traveled across her forehead had worsened these last eleven years. The pain would then escalate as if preparing for an eruption.

"But our children will never inherit this land, Querida. Tío Nazario inherits the Hacienda when Abuelo José dies. Nazario's son inherits after him. The eldest son always inherits the property. That part of Spanish custom will never change."

"I know, Narciso," she softly contended, asking herself how many times will I have to listen to this? "Our son marries soon, and he will oversee his wife's land and property. Remember, the Ballis don't have a son. Our daughters need marriage partners to maintain leagues of land."

"Of course," Narciso rejoined excitedly, "land is an excellent dowry."

He knelt on one knee in front of her. Family relations had received the Land Grants in 1767. "My cousins José Maria and Cayetano got two leagues over twenty years ago, and your Balli kin, Nicolas, and Juan José, also got one."

Maria Ignacia looked up from crocheting, seeking an escape. She felt ill and wished this talk to end. "Please remember, Narciso, our children are young adults. Let's not burden Manuel with your dreams. We owe him and Pilar the finest wedding. She's an only child, and her parents want a gala!"

Custom prescribed that the groom's family paid for all the wedding expenses, including the wedding gown and the trousseau. The Ballis would provide a dowry—no doubt a generous one.

Maria Ignacia knew that Narciso was not interested in listening to talk about wedding plans. Still, on his knee, he gently pulled the needlework from her hands and placed it in the basket.

"Querida," he pressed on, "I want a legacy for our children before I die."

Maria Ignacia's head pounded. She had had enough and pressed her lips into a tight smile. "Before you die, Narciso? You're only forty. We have four children, three are girls, and two are old enough for marriage. How will we find suitable partners if we're out in the middle of, of ...nowhere? The time has not yet come for this, this, dream, and I'm satisfied with that!" She was beginning to stammer, so she pecked Narciso on the cheek, picked up her basket, and left the room.

She entered the salon to check on her daughters' painting lesson, again picked up the lace to crochet, and listened to the tutor's instruction—but she could not focus on his words.

Our family has enjoyed good fortune and happiness because of Narciso's accomplishments. Narciso's hands-on approach to working in la Hacienda was responsible for their prosperity. Maria Ignacia was conflicted. He's the master of the house, and his vision for our future is worthy. As his wife, it was her obligation and duty to submit and support his plan for their future. But I have no knowledge or training in land ownership; how do I prepare? Will we have servants? Neighbors? How about a place to worship?

Narciso descended into a gloom that permeated the entire house each day that passed without a dispatch from the land commissioner. Maria Ignacia blamed herself for his melancholy but continued to pray daily that the authorities would ignore the land request. She'd then console herself; God continues to answer my prayers. Is it a blessing? Yes, it is for me—for all of us. Her education involved applying feminine domestic skills, such as sewing and household management, in an aristocratic Spanish home, and she cultivated these same traditions to her daughters.

She was forty-five years old. The only life she'd known was in haciendas run by household servants—first her parents, then with Narciso. She was used to having family and friends who embraced the happy and the not-so-good times. Their ancestors, the sons of the upper class, had built wealth with vast estates. When they first came from the Old World, they seized opportunities due to their grand notion of entitlement.

She looked up to watch Maria and Francisca painting with quiet intensity while ten-year-old Ignacia concentrated with furrowed brows and her tongue peeking between her teeth. Maria Ignacia smiled and rose to stoop next to her, "Mi Corazón, it's beautiful!" She affectionately referred to her baby as her heart. Maria and Francisca looked at each other and smiled. Their mother was loving and affectionate, constantly touching and hugging her children.

The chapel bell tolled at high noon. Despite the headache, Maria Ignacia would not miss the midday Angelus prayers. She was the spiritual role model to the women in the community who assembled and expected her to attend chapel. She dismissed the tutor and told her daughters, "Get your rosaries and mantillas." They heard Raúl shouting at Narciso as they walked to the nearby chapel.

★

Six wagons piled with cured bales of hay stood outside the stable while Raúl and two vaqueros hauled them in one at a time. Raúl's face was bright red from exertion and straining from the weight of this backbreaking labor. He yelled at Narciso as he exited his home. "¿Que tal, Compadre? Why the late start?"

Narciso approached, frowning and squinting, his mouth tightly shut. He gripped his hands into tight fists. Raúl stopped at his unsmiling face. "Something wrong?"

Narciso hesitated, then replied, "No." He stopped, plucked a piece of hay, and stuck it in his mouth. "Well, yes. I've heard nothing from the commissioner."

Raúl nodded. It was the end of February, and the air was cool, but sweat from the sun and exercise ran down his face. He reached for a bale of hay and stopped. "Why don't you help me? It'll take your mind off of it. Afterward, we can check on the three mares that foaled yesterday. The long ride will do you good, and we'll be home by supper." He again began to haul the bale, hesitated, then said, "But you'll need a horse; Haro took off early this morning like the fires of hell scorching his rear."

Narciso burst out in laughter. "Este caballo es inconformista. He'll always be free-spirited, won't he? And you're going to make sure I earn my keep, aren't you." After a few minutes of hesitation, he shook his head and smiled, "How did that horse get so ornery?"

Raúl, his back bent with a heavy bale, turned towards the stable. "We'll probably find Haro with the mares."

Smiling, Narciso rolled up his sleeves and followed suit.

"I petitioned the King of Spain this time," he panted. "I don't care if it takes another ten years; I'll start a settlement in Tejas, you'll see."

★

Returning from the chapel, Maria Ignacia took Francisca by the hand and said, "I need to lie down. This pain is relentless, and my stomach is upset." Francisca and Ignacia followed her into the bedroom. "Close the curtains, Corazon; the light impales my eyes."

Maria entered with a bowl of chamomile flowers, peppermint oil, and lavender spirits. "Here, Mamá, cover your eyes with this cool cloth." The girls kissed her and closed the door quietly behind them, leaving Maria Ignacia to recover in the darkened room.

It was only for a moment that she had drifted into sleep, but it could have been longer—Maria Ignacia had lost all concept of the past and the present. She removed the cloth from her eyes and tried to sit up slowly. "Jovita!" She reached out with an outstretched hand to touch her savior who'd spared her from death those years ago. Jovita sat serenely, smiling, her face full of light. A spirit?

The pounding in Maria Ignacia's head had subdued. "Jovita, rinse the compress into the bowl and press it over my eyes." She relaxed as the cool, fragrant compress covered her eyes. Her nausea had momentarily passed. The aromatic scent had transported her to those lying-in days when Narciso had sought out Jovita, Maria Ignacia's long-retired childhood nursemaid. He'd even set up a cot for Jovita in their bedroom while he shared Manuel's.

"The headaches began with Ignacia, remember?" Jovita was here, in the room. Wasn't she? "I'd thought I was finished with having babies," she waited, then felt a gentle pressure on the cloth covering her eyes. She's here to heal me. Relaxed, she continued in a hushed tone, "Maria, Francisca, and Manuel were born a year apart, ten months after Narciso and I were married." She giggled, "I must have conceived on my wedding night." She stopped, exhausted from the flashbacks. She dozed, awakened again, removed the cloth, and sought out Jovita, still sitting at the foot of her bed. They smiled at each other. "Jovita, when I was embarazada for the last time, I was so pleased. I knew, finally, this hacienda was home. We couldn't uproot the family, especially a newborn, for an unknown and mysterious land. I'm right, aren't I?" She desperately needed Jovita's response. Suddenly, an overpowering sense of peace filled her.

Maria Ignacia began to reminisce. "Jovita!" She smiled, and the pressure in her brain eased at the thought of the curandera. As a skilled midwife, Jovita's sheer force of will kept her from succumbing to the agony of her labor. "You saved my life!" When her confinement began, she and Narciso knew this childbirth was different. He'd swiftly sought Jovita to assist with her ordeal. "How did he find you, Jovita? We'd heard you'd moved to another settlement." She murmured, "Narciso found you— he knew I needed you."

She looked to the foot of her bed for Jovita, who sat smiling, motionless, and radiant in warmth and light. "Ignacia gave me the most torturous labor of the three. Thank God you caressed my fears with your potions and convinced me this wasn't an abnormal pregnancy." The curandera had massaged her with a balm consisting of the fragrant oils of hyssop, blue tansy, mugwort, and chamomile. Maria Ignacia uncovered her eyes again. She wanted to see that the image sitting with her was indeed Jovita, the short, stocky woman with the strength of a bear. "How long did we walk around the bedroom while you practically carried me?

Jovita, who distracted her from the painful and prolonged labor, wiped her clammy forehead singing low and throaty incantations. By the end of the second day, Maria Ignacia knew that death was imminent and begged for a priest. She couldn't die before arranging last rites and a prompt baptism for herself and this baby.

"You told me that I wasn't going to die. You dared to ignore my pleas for a priest. How did you know?" Instead, Jovita and Narciso had moved Maria Ignacia to an unoccupied one-room jacala that contained a fire pit. Finally, labor began with only a stool and cloth supplies for childbirth. She smiled again toward Jovita, "Remember what you said to me," Maria Ignacia giggled, "you said 'Scream! Yell loud! Curse the devil who brought you to this pain. Nobody can hear, and if they did, they'd understand.'" Maria Ignacia laughed softly, "…and so I screamed."

With gentleness and patience, Jovita had instructed her, "Reach up and hold tight to the post above you, do not let go. I'm here."

"You held me in your powerful arms with every contraction. There I stood, holding on to that post, and you pushed down on my belly with every contraction. I thought I'd die with the violent ones, but you pushed hard with each one."

Maria Ignacia had weakened even more, "I was ready to give up…the pain and the weariness…then you whispered in my ear, 'This is it, one more push,' and the baby came."

She was born at sundown. Maria Ignacia had collapsed onto the bedding on the adobe floor, too exhausted to hear the whimper and wails of a tiny newborn. At the dawn of the fourth day, Jovita placed this tightly wrapped bundle into Maria Ignacia's arms.

"'You have a daughter,' you told me, and I had intense emotions—so much love for this new baby. I named her Maria Ignacia, mi Corazon—

my heart and soul," tears streamed down Maria Ignacia's face as she looked once again at the blurred figure of her beloved nursemaid.

"That morning I attempted to get out of bed, a dagger-like pain pierced my left temple, like today. My stomach turned, and I retched violently. Jovita, you insisted that I lie down; I wasn't yet ready."

She and Narciso moved Maria Ignacia back into the house, making her as comfortable as possible. Jovita then disappeared for three hours and returned with a poultice in which she had wrapped medicinal herbs of cut sage, feverfew plants, chamomile, and a broth made from herbs.

Maria Ignacia laughed at this recollection. "The broth tasted disgusting, but it did relieve nausea and lessened the pounding in my head. I need your broth now, Jovita."

She laid back on her pillow, and her thoughts turned to God. "Does He send these headaches as punishment for not honoring my husband's desire for Tejas?" Although the headaches came monthly, they often began during or after a conversation about Tejas. "I have the freedom to conduct a school to teach the young children the Catholic religion, a needlework social gathering that makes necessary items for the poor. How can I leave all that I've created," she pleaded?"

"I tried to convince Narciso about the importance of potential spouses for our daughters, Jovita; we won't find suitable partners in the wilderness. With Manuel's and Pilar's marriage negotiations complete, I live for this beautiful Catholic wedding. Narciso didn't say anything; he just nodded, Jovita, and said, 'We'll come back here for another wedding or two, Querida. Nothing says that we can't plan weddings for our daughters in Nuevo Leon.'" Francisca opened the door quietly to check on her mother and heard her deep breathing. Maria Ignacia slept.

She woke with a start, Jovita no longer in her room. The pressure across her temple eased, so she removed the wet cloth from her face, reached for additional pillows, and sank deep into their feathery softness. *We need a ceremony—a wedding. One more beautiful and elaborate than the one Narciso and I had twenty-one years ago.*

Through the generations, the parents choose their daughter's marriage partner. Hers, the Hinojosa-Benavides union added prominence and advantages to the Cavazos-González close alliance with the Crown of Spain. Maria Ignacia's father and Don José, Narciso's grandfather, had arranged her union with Narciso, a descendant of King Ferdinand II. Although initially not a love match, youthful intimacy had allowed love and respect to blossom.

She sat up again to dip the compressed pack into the cool water containing the same medicinal herbs Jovita had prepared. She stopped. Jovita, are you here?

Maria Ignacia placed the pack over her eyes and continued to reminisce about the pomp and celebration of her wedding day. Resplendent in an imported gown from Spain, her mother came into her room to give her a blessing, then whispered an odd comment, "A woman is a princess only on her wedding day. After that, she's a servant." Maria Ignacia recalled the words. "I never felt like a servant—I did what I wanted even after we married."

In 1769, Maria Ignacia, twenty-four, and Narciso, nineteen stood in the presence of the bishop of Mexico, who performed the ceremony. She indeed felt like a princess. The bright blue silk dress had three-quarter sleeves finished with ruffled lace engageantes.[2] The richly decorated bodice had a detachable triangular panel of tiny pearls. The petticoat contained an elaborately trimmed matching underskirt visible with an open gown, the skirt made wide by hooped paniers worn underneath with serpentine borders of scalloped lace edged with delicate silk fringe. A low-shaped décolleté edged with a lace ruffle framed Maria Ignacia's neckline, and the edge of a stomacher shaped her tiny waistline. Robings, a gathered ruffled or pleated length of fabric, edged the sides of the open gown, petticoat, and bodice.

The pain had begun to pulsate, and Maria Ignacia pressed her palms against her temple. She concentrated on filling her mind with idyllic memories.

I love even the missteps of that spectacular day! That awful prayer.

After the communion, Maria Ignacia and Narciso exchanged their vows. They sat together at the altar, and the bishop directed her to kneel. He then placed his hand on her head to bless her in this new momentous role. He read the invocation for a faithful and obedient woman. She still remembered parts of the prayer. She remembered thinking that the list seemed endless; whenever the bishop turned the page of the prayer book, he lifted his hand from her head while turning yet another page.

"…let the yoke of marriage to her be one of love and peace. Faithful and chaste, let her marry in Christ. Let her ever follow the model of holy women: …let her strengthen weakness by stern discipline. Let her be grave in demeanor, honorable for her modesty, learned in heavenly doctrine, fruitful in children. Let her life be good and innocent."

Narciso's turn came next; he knelt as she returned to her seat. "Love your wife."

That was it! The duties of a husband held no demands while she must work at becoming a canonized saint! Maria Ignacia smiled; I remember my eyes shot up in disbelief.

Cracking another smile, she thought, Lucky for me, Narciso didn't appear to listen to the blessing. She found joy in her duties as the Doña of her house and partner to the dashingly handsome Narciso. They had a happy and companionable life.

Maria Ignacia felt a tingling on the right side of her face that slowly traveled down her arm. The throb pulsated with each heartbeat. Suddenly a burst of stars erupted behind her eyes. The pounding and the pain ceased. The muscles in Maria Ignacia's arms and legs slackened—the luster in her partially opened eyes vanished; her pupils dilated and fixed.

★

Doña Maria Ignacia lay as if asleep before the altar of her beloved chapel; her body was cleaned and washed with aromatic herbs. Narciso's sister, Teresa, then anointed her with scented olive oil balm mixed with pure myrrh, sweet cinnamon, and calamus to conceal the odor of decomposition.

Maria and Francisca dressed their mother in a black velvet regency gown.

A sheet of fine-spun imported black lace cloaked her body. They wrapped her cut-crystal rosary in her hands that sprinkled diamond-like sparks from the shimmering candles. Around her neck, the daughters draped a heart-shaped locket containing oil- painted miniatures of their deceased grandparents, Maria Ignacia's parents.

Candlelight flickered in the tiny chapel, and shadows quivered across the wooden pews. Fragrances of frankincense, myrrh, and cedar burned in stone bowls scattered throughout.

Overwhelming grief and shock engulfed the family. Maria greeted mourners with shaking hands and stuttering while trying to find the correct response to sympathetic words. Francisca shrank away from the visitors and fussed over Ignacia, whose pale face and wide eyes rebuffed the truth. She sobbed and called out for her Mamá to anyone present.

Manuel's betrothed, Pilar, and her parents came daily to comfort and help with the household tasks. Every day the extended family who took over all chores filled the house.

Narciso would disappear for hours. "I didn't know how ill she was," Narciso said aloud as he walked alongside his beloved horse, Haro. "Nothing feels or sounds the same; it's as if I'm in another world," he mumbled. "She was a strong, vibrant woman; she never complained."

The doctor told Narciso that Maria Ignacia suffered an attack of apoplexy, a suspension of the brain's functions. He based his findings on the symptoms Narciso's daughters described and the swollen grey pallor of her face.

"She died all alone," Narciso choked, and his hands trembled. He swayed and leaned into Haro for support. "Querida, you left too soon. We're not ready for this." He stopped and buried his face against Haro's neck.

People from Monterrey, Real de Santiago de las Sabinas, and the towns and hamlets around Nuevo Leon came to pay their respects. Those who came were the Indios whose children Maria Ignacia faithfully taught catechism, her friends, their families, servants, and relatives. They were young and old, those who either grew up alongside or watched her develop from a young bride into the elegant Doña de Los Cavazos. Revered, the community came in droves to show love and support.

On Sunday, February 28, 1790, the family vault at Real de Santiago de las Sabinas in Nuevo Leon housed the remains of Doña Maria Ignacia. Six professional mourners, las Lloronas, clothed in rough black tunics with attached headcovers remained with the body during the laying out period. Following custom, las Lloronas provided the family relief from mourning and ensured that the body was never alone. Their presence was an expression of Maria Ignacia's standing in the community. After the Requiem mass, las Lloronas led the horse-drawn cart to the burial site chanting the litany of saints, and invocations for the intercession of her soul, while wailing along the way. Narciso, his children, and the mourners walked behind the hearse. At sundown, Las Lloronas, Maria Ignacia's daughters, and close relatives began a ten-day novena for the repose of her soul.

Chapter 5

ONWARD TAMPICO

"How do you know Maria Ignacia died from a brain hemorrhage," I asked Auntie as she sorted through her dresses. "It's horrible— unimaginable that she died at forty-five." Daddy was sixty-two when he died, and I thought he was too young.

Auntie ignored my question, then nodded, "This one." She turned in my direction, holding in front of her a two-piece frog button-suit dress. "What do you think?"

The outfit was lovely and elegant. "The color is alabaster," Auntie informed me of the pale, almost white cotton and acetate jacket and skirt. "Today, we'll maneuver the border, so dress with style. You don't have a birth certificate, and I want a distraction for those men behind the counter."

I hadn't learned how to attract attention, but Auntie made me feel like I could. Her words sounded as if it was easy. I never saw myself as a distraction, but then, maybe she meant herself to be the one to distract. I looked in the closet for my fashion possibilities.

"A customs agent might overlook a birth certificate when he sees style and splendid, good looks," Auntie said optimistically.

While Auntie's clothes came from Bloomingdales, mine consisted of the hand-made variety—simple A-line mini dresses popularized in the 1960s by the fashion model Twiggy. They were easy to sew, and I'd make several styles from one pattern. I chose a wine-colored A-line dress with a printed sheer voile overlay and flared ¾ sleeves. The hem barely touched the top of my knees.

A list of clothing dos and don'ts came with the dorm resident's acceptance. I initially purchased an array of white garter belts that I later dyed to match bras and panties after the white garments turned dingy. Trousers were forbidden on campus, a common theme in all girls' Catholic schools. Not a problem; I didn't even own a pair. Classroom attire required wearing stockings, not socks. Only a one-piece bathing suit was permitted when using the campus pool, and an acceptable gym item was a one-piece tennis dress with attached shorts; I took the one we used in the high school gym.

My only luxury was shoes. I had a surgically fused right ankle, and only a flat-wide Mary Jane or Weejuns loafer accommodated my feet comfortably.

She applied a finishing touch of fire-engine red lipstick.

"You make a statement with this!" and handed it to me to apply. "Give me your identification," Auntie said as we entered the car. "My driver's license and the fall semester's registration papers."

Minutes later, Auntie eased into the International Border Crossing and parked her flashy car as close to the big window of the building as possible.

"Someone will be watching," she remarked as we emerged from the car and headed for the door.

No one else was in line—we were the early birds. The scent of coffee permeated, and I realized that this group of agents was probably on a first shift.

"Let me do all the talking but follow my lead. We need tourist permits, and I must register the car because we're going more than 26 miles past the border."

"Okay," I uttered, feeling a little bit queasy.

I remembered the crossings from childhood—just as daunting as this one was today. Uniformed men, hats lowered and rifles on their shoulders, walked back and forth, suspiciously eyeing incoming vehicles.

"Don't worry," Auntie appeased, "your license and school papers will be enough."

Auntie somehow felt she could get the document that would allow me to enter with her into the interior of Mexico. My fingers and toes tingled in anticipation; I hated being the focus of attention!

She pulled me close, smiled at the young customs agent, and looked straight into his eyes.

The agent's eyes lingered on her vehicle while Auntie pointed to it parked outside the window. She took my hand, "Necesitamos visas, y un permiso para mi auto. "We need visas and a permit for my car."

"Papeles," the officer replied hastily, and Auntie handed him the documents.

He scrutinized the papers and then began reading the school's registration paper.

Auntie talks, attempting to distract him. "Qué suerte que puedes leer Inglés. Me parece que la mayoría de los estadounidenses no pueden escribir español mucho menos leerlo. What luck you can read English. I'm afraid that most Americans can't write Spanish much less read it."

My mouth was dry, and my heart began to palpitate. I hoped Auntie was correct and that the agent was not feeling demeaned.

In perfect English, the agent looked up, smiled, and replied, "I graduated from St. Joseph's Academy in Brownsville."

Auntie looked at his paper name tag. "Manuel," she accentuated his name. "You just brightened my day with a burst of brilliant sunshine!" She raised her hands and wiggled her fingers to indicate a flurry.

He shook his head slightly and shyly asked, "Does she have her birth certificate?"

I focused on him, attempting eye contact, but he looked away quickly. Before I could answer, Auntie babbled, "I picked her up at school for a surprise trip to Tampico."

"You're traveling to Tampico?" He looked at my driver's license and then went back to me. I smiled again, and he once again hastily looked away.

"You're from Galveston and go to school in San Antonio?" He avoided eye contact by looking at my driver's license.

"Yes," I replied, "I just completed my first year."

"She's studying to be a doctor," Auntie interrupted again, "and I want her to have some fun before returning to her studies. You know all work and no play?"

That queasy feeling turned into a stomach flip-flop. I closed my eyes and took a deep breath.

He smiled again and inserted the paper into the typewriter. The whole time he typed, Auntie kept up a lively chatter, waved her hands, and, to my horror, began getting personal.

"Manuel, are you married?"

I felt sick; if he said no, she would indicate I was single.

"No," he replies.

I almost swallowed my tongue.

She leaned forward and whispered, "You have a sweetheart, right? A handsome young man like yourself probably has more than one."

Manuel appeared to shrink, and I fought the impulse to bolt. Auntie sensed the discomfort and changed the subject to her husband, Diaz.

"I was only sixteen, much younger than you are now," she waited for a reaction; sensing that, he looked up and nodded.

"My cousins and I loved dances, so my Tía, along with the other neighbor women with daughters, would walk us to the pier on Galveston beach, where the musicians met with their instruments. The matrons remained seated in portable chairs, watching the young men, especially the soldiers."

Manuel concentrated on his fingers typing.

"We were young girls who just wanted to dance. The musicians played traditional Mexican songs, el Jarabe Tapatío or Las Chiapanecas." She waited for Manuel to respond. When he didn't, she continued. "You know, the one where the caballeros dance with their hands behind their back and las chicas sway their skirts back and forth?"

Manuel looked up, avoiding eye contact; he nodded again, and she kept on.

"I saw this gorgeous blue-eyed soldier standing by the refreshment table and asked him to dance. The attraction was instant, and the rest is history."

Manuel stopped and looked at Auntie with an expression that seemed to say he was not surprised.

He handed her the documents and reminded her to have the car inspected.

I rushed for the door grabbing Auntie by the arm.

"I can't believe you told him I was studying to be a doctor," I whispered, dashing to get outside.

"Why not? You're studying Biology. Pre-med students take Biology."
"I'm not a pre-med student. I'm a Biology major."

"What's the difference?"

I rolled my eyes and let it go.

The inspector stood by the car, and Auntie handed him her car document. However, this agent appeared mesmerized. I again held my breath, silently appealing to God that she'd behave.

"¿Que Tal? How are you?" Auntie looked at his paper badge, "Raúl."

They reviewed the vehicle's every detail; the new grillwork in a 1967 GTO. She pushed the button to open the top and pulled open the hood. Both stared in awe at the engine.

"Es un motor V-8 de 400 pulgadas cúbicas. It's a 400 cubic inch V-8 engine." Auntie bragged.

After a quick signature, the inspector whistled and handed back the document tipping his hat with his hand.

I relaxed, and we were finally on our way. Auntie waved and gave the inspector a mock salute as she exited.

"You okay?" Auntie laughed and, after a moment's hesitation, "We have over 400 kilometers (km) to Tampico," she switched the speed gauge to kilometers. It was eight a.m. Saturday. Auntie had picked me up in San Antonio on Thursday. So far, we'd spent our nights in the beach town of Port Isabel and Harlingen the next day.

Tonight, we'll be in Tampico.

"I figure if we make one stop and all goes well, we'll be entering the city limits around three p.m."

She looked to me for a response.

"Okay with me," I replied. I was along for the ride and the adventure.

After 25 km, a barrier blocked our progress with Alto! A sign indicated "Tampico" via Highway 101 past the inspection point. Two stern-faced men in military gear stood akimbo at this check station, moving their hands to their rifles. One held up his hand and stepped in front of the car.

"¡Papeles! Papers!"

Auntie handed them over. As he checked, the other guard approached the car and slowly walked around, peering into the back seat.

Auntie watched him. I hoped she sensed that now was not the time for reckless conversation.

"¡Abre el castaño! Open the trunk!" he commanded. Auntie pushed the button.

He peered, closed it, approached his partner, and leaned towards him, whispering something.

The guard handed Auntie our papers and stated, "No tenemos muchas mujeres viajando solas por aquí. We don't have many women traveling alone."

"Este es mi país de nacimiento y me encanta conducir a través de él. I'm in my birth country and I love driving through it." Auntie replied with a smile.

They nodded and waved us through. "Buen viaje, cuidado. Have a good trip and be careful."

Relief washed over me again. Thirty minutes later, we drove alongside the ocean, its waters sparkling like a prism from rising sun rays.

I looked at the map and the state in which Tampico resided. "The state of Tamaulipas appears as large as Texas."

"Look again," Auntie remarked, "it resembles an elephant sitting on its 'hiney' with his long trunk in the air."

I laughed, "You're right!"

The road was lonely, with only seagulls and pelicans for company. "It looks as if we're going through marshland. What'll we do if we need to use the restroom? On a visit to Monterrey, we had to pay a dime to the attendant to use the public facility and toilet paper."

"We'll just stop at the brushwood," Auntie pointed. She reached behind my seat and handed me a bag with toilet paper, washcloths, and a soap bar.

"I have it covered," she smiled triumphantly.

"Oh gosh! Mama would never pee in the bushes, but that's okay!" We laughed.

"Tila was always a bit prissy." She added quickly, "But that's not a bad thing."

We were silent for a while; I leaned back and closed my eyes. With the convertible top-down, I felt the breeze playing with my hair. The salty smell of the ocean prickled my nostrils.

"Did you know that Hernán Cortés founded Veracruz searching for gold?" Auntie began. "That's when it became a port city and the most important port of entry in Mexico."

"Did your mother Lucia, my grandmother, and your dad have relatives that stayed after Cortés? Why did they choose Veracruz?" is that why they went there?" I sat up straight.

It seemed strange that they'd travel far away for a love nest.

"It could be Mama Lucia had distant relations there, but I don't know. My father was from Ireland, where he left a wife when he came to this country. I was two when he died."

Occasionally during family gatherings, I'd stay close enough to listen while the aunts talked about their mother, Lucia, and her lover, Auntie's father, Dr. Séamos Manus. The story was now a family legend. On New Year's Day in 1901, Dr. Manus was returning home after an hours-long house call when approached by two men. After a short conversation that included shouting, one of the men shot him. They escaped, but the story developed that the men were Dr. Manus' brothers-in-law who came from Ireland to persuade him to return to their sister, Dr. Manus's wife, in Ireland. She lived in limbo, having been married in the Catholic Church and unable to have a life that included children. Dr. Manus refused, and his death allowed the widow Manus another opportunity to marry.

"My beginnings are a tragic tale," Auntie mused.

It appeared that we were the only ones driving for miles on the highway. The scenery consisted of flat landscape with unremarkable structures, if that's what they were, far into the distance. Sometimes we'd pass acres upon acres of flourishing cornfields. An occasional truck driver going in the opposite direction would honk and wave; Auntie would follow suit.

"Is Tampico a big tourist destination?" I asked. The only Mexican state my parents took us to visit was Nuevo Leon, the same place Auntie talked about in Narciso's story.

Auntie shrugged. "Don't know. Never been."

We stopped to stretch our legs and examined our surroundings.

Habitation didn't seem to exist—just bare land. Auntie raised the car's top and turned on the radio which emitted nothing but static. I pulled a cassette from my bag and held it up.

"Nothing depressing," she said, making a face.

"It's Sgt Pepper's Lonely-Hearts Club Band. The Beatles," Auntie nodded yes. I inserted the cassette, and the tunes began. I lowered the volume so we could talk.

"How did people travel to Tampico? I mean, how did Grandmother Lucia and Dr. Manus—you said twelve hours by car—did they go by horse and buggy? I had a fanciful notion of Lucia and her lover packing up a covered wagon with their belongings.

"By train, maybe?" Auntie replied. "I never asked my mother." She scrunched her face as if trying to remember an incident.

"I don't know. That could have counted as a honeymoon if the lovers traveled by wagon. But they most likely hopped on a train for a quicker escape from Runge."

It was close to noon, and we'd been on the road for three hours. "We're gonna have to stop soon."

"Uh oh," I said, "potty time?"

"Find us a place," Auntie said urgently.

I spotted a tiny town on the map. "Keep an eye out for Guemez."

A few minutes later, a crude sign on a wooden stake with Guemez appeared; it was a sharp right turn.

Auntie screeched the car to a halt and shrugged, "It's this or the bushes."
"Let's stop," I concurred.

We turned into a dirt road and came upon a hamlet of three gaily painted thatched-roof huts with flimsy clapboard siding. One had an opened screen door, and Auntie parked at this entrance. She raised the convertible's top. The vehicle's tires had kicked up the dry dirt, and combined with the warm air, I began to sneeze. I spotted a massive field of corn in the distance and wondered what other air- borne irritants might rouse my allergies.

"Let's see what kind of trouble we can get into," Auntie stepped eagerly onto the porch.

We entered a hall that appeared to serve as a multipurpose room. A counter like those in small grocery stores held fresh fruits and vegetables, cans of Spam, and various sodas ready for purchase. Behind the counter stood a short, sturdy brown woman with long black braids. She wore a white smock with a beautiful multi-colored shawl across her shoulders. She smiled and nodded, carefully arranging bags of chicharónes into a large basket as we looked around.

A battered table with four questionable chairs was in the corner of the room near a window. Catty-corner, stacked benches lined the wall.

I looked for a bathroom, but the only other room was a kitchen emitting the aromas of spices, onion, garlic, and whatever else was cooking in a large cast-iron cauldron in the opened fire pit built into the wall.

"That must be a kitchen," Auntie whispered, "Let's get a bite to eat."

"¿Nos servirás lo que estás cocinando? Will you serve us whatever you're cooking?"

The woman asked us to sit, and Auntie asked, "¿Tiene un baño?" She murmured, "I really have to go, don't you?"

The woman smiled and signaled for us to follow. She walked behind the building toward the cornfield. Auntie and I looked at each other. I felt the pulse of my heartbeat and wondered if Auntie was also apprehensive.

"Where are we going?" I mumbled; the need to use the restroom was now urgent. I'm so much more comfortable with people in a noisy city.

"¿Vamos al baño?" Auntie hollered at the woman ahead, "Are we going to the restroom?"

She nodded and waved her hand to follow.

"She understands but doesn't speak," I whispered. "Am I the only one who thinks this is creepy?"

"She's taking us to the sacrifice," Auntie joked. I didn't laugh.

We neared the cornfield, and the woman stopped and whistled. Auntie and I froze. After several minutes, a woman who looked like a twin version of our guide emerged from the tall stalks.

The two engaged in an unrecognizable conversation. "She speaks another language," I whispered to Auntie. "Maybe it's their dialect," Auntie pointed out.

The twin took us across the field, away from the cornfield. In the distance, we saw a pig pen and cattle grazing on an emerald patch of grass. I was frightened once again and looked at Auntie for a cue. I saw her eyes dart back and forth, alert to any danger signs.

We approached a six-foot-high pen of stacked brush and tree branches. An acrid, recognizable odor drifted from the opening. Twin turned, smiled, and gestured for us to enter. She reached deep into her ample pocket and, with an outstretched arm, handed us a roll of toilet paper.

Auntie and I looked at each other and entered. The stench was so overpowering that I forced myself to take shallow breaths. Up and out in record time, Auntie tossed me the toilet paper and hollered, "I'll wait outside."

Crouching was problematic. Even with corrective surgery, I had problems squatting and needed hands to hold on to something. My legs lacked the strength to scrunch for even a minute. I wasted time looking for a spot where I could use my hands for stability but found nothing. Breathing in noxious smells became the focus of my intense discomfort, so I proceeded to the far corner, squatted halfway, and emptied my bladder. While holding on to the toilet paper, I attempted to raise my underpants with one hand. Then, I heard noises like dry brushes breaking. Thinking Auntie was playing a joke, I called her, but the sound came from this side, near me, opposite the entrance—just next to where I squatted. I stuck the toilet paper under my chin so I could use both hands to pull up my underpants when an unexpected head pushed through the brush and blared a loud mooo!

I collided with Auntie on the way out.

★

"You drive," Auntie threw me the keys to her GTO. I was thrilled. She hugged a large Mexican Mercado bag of chicharónes, ripped open a bag, and began eating. She appeared as delighted as a child. I was apprehensive about driving this vehicle. I assumed control by first adjusting the seat and mirrors. Before I inserted the keys into the ignition, I reminded myself to remain focused and alert.

"It won't explode," Auntie reassured me.

"It's not that," I said defensively, "I've never driven a car with such a powerful engine; Mama's car is a small Chevy."

I tapped on the gas, and the car shot forward. I braked, and the momentum threw us toward the dash. I took a deep breath. Auntie laughed and continued crunching. "It has a personality; I did the same thing when I first got it."

Her comment calmed me, and I took it even slower while maneuvering the car onto the dirt road. We made our way toward the highway, dust whirling in our wake.

★

The cracked windows allowed for some air, but the pungent smell of chili permeated the interior within a half-hour. I marveled at Auntie's appetite for this snack.

"Want some?" she shoved the bag under my chin.

"Nnnnno!" I eased the bag back. It may be that chicharónes are the one Mexican food that I detest. The tangy smell made me gag.

"Can we put the top down?" I needed air.

Auntie waved her hand for me to pull over. She smacked her lips, licked her fingers, and leaned toward me to push the button. I eased back onto the highway.

"I grew up with chicharónes," she mentioned. "Mama Lucia made them from scratch as a wholesome snack for my brothers and sisters."

I inwardly grimaced. A good snack made from the skin of slaughtered pigs!

The 180 Gulf Coast highway marker guided our lane toward Tampico. After a quarter-hour, we spotted a sign for a town called La Zamorina.

"Look!" I pointed, "We could've stopped here had we known it was so close. I bet they have toilet facilities."

Auntie burst out in laughter. I was surprised she didn't choke. "The food in Guemez was delicious, and the hospitality superb. What's not to like?" She leaned forward, giving a deep belly laugh.

"It was hard to enjoy the moment after the unexpected visitor startled me while using the so-called toilet."

Auntie laughed so hard that tears rolled down her face. I looked at her red, wet face and couldn't help but chuckle.

"It's a moment you'll always remember," she gushed into her handkerchief. "I'm well acquainted with inconveniences growing up using outhouses."

"And cows barging in?"

We laughed.

The map showed that Hwy 80 was our route, and we passed the town of Villa Manuel, an hour away from Tampico. Towns appeared regularly; Altamira, 17 km, and Miramar, 8 km.

We entered Tampico in the early evening.

"The first order of business is finding a hotel," Auntie looked at the ads on the map.

We were on the outskirts of Tampico, passing ramshackle businesses with signs advertising a mechanic, a tire shop, and many restaurants.

"Let's go downtown."

After ten minutes, traffic slowed, and we eased toward the town's center.

"Wow, it's beautiful!" Downtown was a magical district, filled with buildings encased in wrought iron, the homes reminding me of the antebellum architecture of Galveston.

"It looks more like New Orleans than Mexico," Auntie noted.

We circled the blocks looking for a hotel.

"Walking will be a nice change of pace," Auntie commented.

We passed the Plaza de Centro Libertad, the downtown square.

"Misión Tampico!" Auntie pointed to a structure that resembled the Alamo in San Antonio.

I turned toward its entrance and parked in the courtyard. We entered the door marked Oficina.

Auntie asked for a room with two beds. The porter took our luggage to a charming room with twin beds and a small bathroom.

"What a luxurious hotel," I remarked to Auntie, who smiled in agreement.

"I saw a restaurant next door; let's eat, then walk to the Immaculate Conception Cathedral."

"You think your baptismal certificate is there?"

"I hope. The church was erected in the mid-1800s, and I was born in 1899. If my baptismal certificate is anywhere, it's there." She wrinkled her brow and bit her lip.

"It'll be there," I pronounced optimistically.

★

Auntie barely talked and picked at her food. She appeared far away in her thoughts. After dinner, we strolled the avant-garde historic main street lined with novelty shops, boutiques, restaurants, salons, and galleries. We continued to El Metro, the town center, and passed the Huasteca Museum.

"Tomorrow, when it's open, let's visit this place," Auntie suggested.

We stood in awe at the magnificent Immaculate Conception Cathedral across the Plaza de Armas. Auntie whispered, "All babies deserve a baptism here."

The church was locked, and as we started back to the hotel, we heard music from the plaza, a happy, upbeat tempo. Young and old had gathered to enjoy the Mexican spirit of a fiesta. Children were running around and playing, while nearby, abuelos and abuelas, the guardians of the young, kept their eyes on their grandchildren so their parents could dance. "It's a typical Saturday night fandango," Auntie took my hand, face shining. I felt my heart thumping with excitement—there was no place like a dance floor that freed my inhibitions. Dancing partners at college dances gave me the confidence that I was appealing, approachable, and adept on the dance floor.

We stepped into the crowd, and before long, we were wrapped up in the boisterous revelry. Different musicians played, which added to the diversity. A new group began a traditional Mexican corrido, a nostalgic song, and the crowd, including Auntie, joined in the singing. In the next song, "La Puerta Negra," the singer wailed an account of a forbidden romance.

Auntie began dancing with the others and howled with the musicians.

Her pleasure was contagious, and I joined her on the crowded dance floor. The band followed with a catchy tune, "Y Llegaste Tú," a life transformed by love, and we loudly sang along.

Two Caballeros approached Auntie. "Hola, Señora, me llamo Franco, y este es mi amigo, Miguel. Hello ma'am, my name is Franco, and this is my friend, Miguel."

We introduced ourselves. Auntie mentioned that we were traveling from Texas, and they informed us that they spoke English. Auntie asked if they lived in Tampico.

"No," Franco answered, "we're recent graduates from the Centro de Estudios Avanzados de las Américas in Monterrey and were traveling around Mexico for the summer.

Franco and Miguel were quick to smile, confident, and self-assured. They were very handsome and reminded me of the actors in the movie Reportaje, with Pedro Infante and Jorge Negrete. John and I saw it with our dad at the Azteca Cine, the only Mexican cinema in Galveston.

"We just want to dance," they told Auntie, looking at me. Most of the women in the plaza seemed to have escorts. Do you mind if we dance with your daughter?"

"She's my niece, and we're both here to dance!" she responded emphatically.

We laughed, and the music began again—the story of "La Chona" about a woman whose life was bearable only when dancing, crooned through the loudspeakers. We danced the polka with our new partners, circling the crowded floor.

Franco offered to buy beer after three delightful dances.

"No, thank you," Auntie responded politely. She pulled me to a stand selling bottled soft drinks while I watched Franco and Miguel head toward the beer stand.

A woman approached the microphone and began a powerful rendition of "Tú Sólo Tú," a classic ballad about a passionate love affair. Auntie and I sat on the low brick fence that surrounded the plaza. When this song finished, the music changed to a lively cumbia mix.

"We'll leave after I dance one more," Auntie said, shaking and shimmying her shoulders. "Come join me."

"As soon as I finish my drink," I assured her.

Some of the people dancing raised one hand in the air and placed the other on their midsection, and Auntie followed suit. She danced the folkloric steps of the cumbia, my favorite dance because it doesn't require a partner. I watched her and the others while I sipped my drink. I remembered the long, delightful day and felt myself unwinding after the long drive. I watched as Auntie blended in with the other dancers. I marveled at her grace and agility as she flowed with the changes in rhythm, her gestures sensual and seductive. It's a long piece, and Auntie danced with complete abandon. The tempo shifted yet again. She twirled and shimmied her shoulders harmoniously with the music, wholly engaged in a floor packed with dancers. A couple bumped into her, and she moved away, spinning, the full-skirted dress she'd changed into swirling around her.

Then, her underwear dropped to the ground. Auntie didn't wear the cotton body-fitting briefs that were the fashion. No, she wore the 1930s silky long-legged bloomers. I watched in horror and felt the color drain from my face. However, Auntie kicked the garment under a bench with utmost grace and finesse. I squeezed through the crowd of dancers to join her, my mind spinning. Do I retrieve or leave them? Auntie, who hadn't missed a beat, smiled, and shrugged. She held out her hands for me to join her. I turned toward the bench, and Auntie pulled on my arm. After twenty minutes, the music ended, and the crowds dispersed.

"Leave it; I have plenty more. Besides, it'll give the groundskeepers something to talk about tomorrow."

★

The lights were out in our room, and Auntie and I were quiet and still. I was profoundly happy. I once again mused over the fabulous day, one more exciting than when Mama took John and me to Disneyland in

California when it first opened.

Auntie was phenomenal; adventurous, fearless, expressive, and hilarious. I hadn't known what awaited when we began at the border. I was afraid that Auntie might have to change her plans because of me. Then came the unexpected events in Guemez with the outhouse and the cow. Following that, we embraced our roots with familiar dances and songs. Electricity charged through me when I thought about the handsome Caballeros. Last, the grand finale, underpants, a salacious fantasy for the plaza sentry. I began to giggle, hands over my mouth so as not to disturb Auntie. She heard me and began to giggle too. We sat up from our beds and convulsed in laughter.

Chapter 6

AN ENDING AND A NEW BEGINNING

We both sat up in bed, wide awake and laughing so hard my sides hurt.

"The look on your face was priceless," Auntie said, snorting and giggling. "If you think losing my drawers is scandalous, I will tell you a shocker of a story that began after Maria Ignacia's funeral."

I was fully awake, and I immediately fluffed my pillow and sat straight up. She had my undivided attention.

★

A permanent spring named Ojo de Agua gave rise to the town of Real de Santiago de las Sabinas in Mexico. Here is where the Cavazos family established its New World roots. The water's source arose from the spiraling mountain's underground streams that fed it. It has always been the wellspring of a thriving community. It was an oasis surrounded by Montezuma Bald Cypress trees, sacred to native people whose wood was used for sturdy house beams and furniture.

The Montezuma Bald Cypress is a large evergreen with weeping branches and spiral leaves. It spritzes the air with the smell of sweet pine or peppery juniper depending on the season. At high noon, a species of bird that inhabit the mature deciduous forest, the chachalacas, escaped the hot sun and gathered upon the branches, their noisy chatter carrying for miles during a breezy spring day.

In 1790, the utilities of this tree became part of the culture of the residents currently living in the area. The fast-growing Montezuma Bald Cypress reached seventy feet in thirty years with a canape spread of thirty feet. Its bark peeled into strips. The Indians called the ancient-looking base Ahuehuete, which means "upright drum in water" or "old man of the water." Curanderas and native healers used its resin to treat gout complaints, ulcers, wounds, toothaches, and bronchitis.

★

Guadalupe remained at the Hacienda during the mourning period to help her young cousins, Narciso's children, Maria, Francisca, Ignacia, and José Manuel. At seventeen, she's elder only to eleven-year-old Ignacia. A spirited and light-hearted young woman, she was the delight of her family, especially her father, who was Narciso's uncle. She lodged at Narciso's house with the best intentions—to help with the household, to guide the traffic of mourners who continued to come daily, but primarily, out of kindness for little Ignacia, whose grief was profound. She thoughtfully prepared Ignacia treats to fortify her appetite, and small sewing gifts she backstitches for strength and durability.

"I made a blanket, Ignacia, using the material from some of your Mamá's dresses," she draped the blanket over her shoulders. Ignacia held the fabric to her face, breathing in her mother's fragrance.

With Guadalupe's presence in the household, something else was happening. Whenever she and Narciso were in the same room, they generated sparks and excitement. They'd sneak glances at each other. She'd wait at a window or hover near a door in anticipation of Narciso's entrance at any moment. When no one was looking, Narciso would stroke her cheek, or they'd touch their foreheads together. Every evening before she retired to the guest bedroom, she'd hug each family member, but with Narciso, the embrace lasted longer, and they'd melt into each other—or so it seemed to Maria, Narciso's eldest. On the ninth day of devotional prayers for the repose of Maria Ignacia's soul, which marked the end of the novena, Guadalupe and Narciso whispered to each other about meeting at Ojo de Agua before her return home. They both wanted a chance to be alone.

The forest of Ojo de Agua was a perfect place to meander or meditate, its pathways covered in abundant vegetation giving a wounded spirit a sense of calmness. The tree trunk's base near the water's edge provided a natural bench for solitary contemplation—or romantic whispers. It was here, encircled by the branches of one of the ancient trees hidden from the view of a pedestrian, that Narciso and Guadalupe began their encounters. Embarking on a forbidden love affair, they spoke softly, exchanging words of endearment, tenderness, and desire.

They talked for hours, meeting daily for another two weeks.

"This is all a dream," Narciso whispered to Guadalupe. "I keep thinking I'm away on a cattle drive, and you are home waiting for me."

Narciso wrapped his hands around one of hers. "I don't know how to comfort my children. This world would become meaningless and overwhelming if it weren't for you."

They sat facing each other, and Guadalupe inched closer, their clothing clumsily stashed in the bushes.

"It's okay, Narciso, she whispered soothingly, "everything you feel is just nature's way of letting in as much as you can manage. Your daughters have each other, and Manuel has Pilar."

Narciso looked at her, his eyes illuminated, "I would not have been able to get through this misery without you."

"We belong together," Guadalupe whispered. "You need someone strong always to be there to comfort you."

Narciso and Guadalupe surrendered to passion. Every time they made love, Narciso's feelings became more intense. For the first time in his life, he was passionately in love and did not doubt that Guadalupe loved him as intensely.

"You are my first love," he said, "we picked each other, and we'll stay together forever. Nothing else exists when we're alone."

At their subsequent encounter, Narciso told Guadalupe, "Raúl warned me that the children are beginning to suspect that something is going on between us."

"How?" Guadalupe, at first, appeared alarmed, then changed her tone, "Except for Ignacia, they aren't children, Narciso, they are young adults," and a hint of a smile touched the tips of her lips as she expressed, "Every girl dreams of romantic interludes."

"I'm absent from home for stretches at a time. What am I expected to do—pace from room to room, touching Maria Ignacia's keepsakes?" Francisca told Raúl today that she hasn't yet seen me grieving.

Guadalupe cuddled close to Narciso, who quickly forgot the conversation.

"Come live with me," Narciso whispered. "With you in the spare room, it'll be easier to come together."

"Papá will be home soon from his cattle drive, and it won't be easy to get away," she answered. "We cannot live together—not without marriage."

★

A serious matter was at hand that further complicated the relationship.

Guadalupe was Narciso's first cousin. This degree of consanguinity prohibited a marriage embedded in Catholic Canon law. Only the pope possessed the power of dispensation. Narciso would have to pay a hefty mordida, the bite, a euphonism to describe the bribe or kickback that would initiate the steps in granting permission.

Narciso began regular visits with his aunt and uncle, Tía Maria, and Tío Francisco, who initially warmly welcomed Narciso's social calls. Tía and Tío opened their home as a haven for their beloved nephew after his wife's tragic passing. "His home must be full of tortuous memories of Maria Ignacia," they told each other. Gradually they became aware that Guadalupe's and Narciso's behavior was not one of the primo hermanos, relatives who shared common grandparents. They were horrified! In their eyes, the relationship was incestuous and subject to social stigma because first cousins shared a bond not unlike one of a brother and sister. Their beloved daughter and nephew were a couple doomed to the fires of Hell.

Tío rebuked Narciso, his face red with rage, "Guadalupe is just a child, and you've ruined her! She will never have a wedding, and you, Narciso, have disgraced our family!" Tío Franciso then revealed the bombshell, "Guadalupe is pregnant, and you, Narciso, are responsible!"

★

In 1790, Narciso buried his first wife, Maria Ignacia, but in his grief, he began an intimate relationship with his first cousin, Guadalupe, who readily reciprocated his affections. She was now pregnant, and Narciso's daughters avoided contact with him whenever he was around. They were embarrassed and confused, asking each other— "Did Papá ever love Mamá? Do they act like lovers around other people? Can other people see what's going on?

"She's almost your age," Maria de los Santos mentioned to Francisca. "How could Papá bring us this scandal?" The girls with their youngest sister, Ignacia, hastened to the chapel for prayers, a daily habit their mother practiced. Manuel made himself scarce by escaping the turmoil at the hacienda with more extended visits to Tejas with his betrothed Pilar.

The tumultuous year mercifully ended with Guadalupe's first child, a second son for Narciso whom they named Jorge. Now more than ever, Narciso was obligated to hasten the dispensation, which required additional mordidas.

"It's all very complicated," the padre told Narciso looking down at his sandals while shuffling his feet, "the bishop of Monterrey must submit the request to the Pope. The bishop cannot, of his right, grant dispensation. Only the Pope can permit a subordinate to officiate."

"What's taking so long? It's been many months, and Guadalupe's father is threatening to move the family away," Narciso exclaimed, shoulders raised, hands splayed, and eyes pleading.

"Prayers and the guidance of reputable authors who know canon law. They must determine if God will favor the dispensation."

Exasperated with the negotiations, Narciso reminded the padre, "The request for dispensation has already gone to Monterrey!"

"Then, the bishop will send the dispensation request to Mexico City," the padre concluded, raising his hand to wave a blessing.

Narciso attempted to persuade with another revelation, "Guadalupe was again emparazada."

"Another pregnancy," the padre's eyes bulged. In a shaky voice, he replied, "The bishop, if he is so inclined, may then deem the marriage a matter of moral necessity," he shook his head and hastily waved his hand, leaving Narciso standing in the vestibule.

★

In 1791, Manuel and Pilar's wedding was a gala event that brought all the surrounding families together. Narciso's and Maria Ignacia's daughters served as three of the dozen bridesmaids at the wedding party. Narciso attended with Guadalupe, not yet showing her pregnancy, and carrying baby Jorge. Following the three-day celebration, Manuel and Pilar left for the Balli's pastureland called "Padre Island," granted by the Spanish Crown in 1767. At the year's end, Guadalupe delivered a girl whom they named Clara.

Narciso and Guadalupe continued their secret meetings overcoming obstacles with the help of her mother, Narciso's Tía.

"The children enchant Mamá," Guadalupe giggled as she snuggled into Narciso's arms. Tía Maria adored her grandbabies. Her assistance allowed Guadalupe freedom for Narciso's company.

Narciso was invigorated with his beautiful young Guadalupe. She was vivacious and energetic; her mind stimulated by the wonders of pregnancy.

"You are the perfect partner to be by my side when we leave our haciendas for the land in Tejas," he whispered. "Then we can put all the gossip behind us."

Guadalupe stood, pushing away, "Did you get the notice, the dispensation?"

"No, no," he responded quickly, "but soon—I feel it," he looked at her anxious face.

"Without marriage, Narciso, I will not flaunt our relationship any more than we already do. Papá is threatening to move to a hacienda near Matamoros. We can only be together because Papá is gone, and Mamá pretends she doesn't see what's happening between us."

★

Life moved on, and in July 1792, a local Nuevo Leon landowner, Blas Garza of Hacienda La Mote, asked Narciso for Francisca's hand in marriage.

"Maria and Ignacia are the only ones left at home, and they'll be married before I get that dispensation," Narciso complained to Raúl.

"At least Maria can take care of Ignacia. She's barely thirteen," Raúl responded, "don't give up." He paused, then, with a smirk, asked Narciso, "Have you paid enough mordida?"

"If the deliberations take much longer," Narciso answered, kicking his boot against the dirt, "I won't have anything left to start that community in Tejas except for pickaxes and mules."

"Ah, yes, Tejas," Raúl repeated and nodded back and forth.

Then, in late summer, Narciso received the notice. He could not wait to tell Guadalupe. In haste, he forgot to greet his aunt and uncle and pushed past them at the doorway, calling for Guadalupe. She entered apprehensively, holding Clara while Jorge tugged at her skirt. She looked first to her parents instead of Narciso, who shrugged their shoulders, indicating they didn't understand why Narciso was so excited.

"Is the dispensation for the marriage official?" Tío asked in hopes of relief from the scandalous ordeal.

Narciso ignored him and took Guadalupe's free hand.

"Sit down, mi Cariña, my love; I have fantastic news! Tía's face softened with a smile as she gazed at the lovers. Narciso pulled out a letter and read it aloud.

On this day, February 22, 1792, His Majesty, Charles IV of Spain, grants to José Narciso Cavazos 79 leagues of property in Spanish Tejas so named El Agostadero de San Juan de Carricitos.[3]

"This document," Narciso waved the paper over his head, "guarantees that we'll get the dispensation," he looked toward his uncle, hoping that the news had pacified him.

Chapter 7

TAMPICO SUNDAY

I was in that stage of sleep just before wakefulness dreaming of sitting at beautiful Ojo de Agua at the water's edge with my legs submerged. My mother and aunts sat under the giant Montezuma Bald Cypress trees surrounding the lake. We had been visiting family in Sabinas Hidalgo, our vacation spot, whenever Daddy needed his Mexican recreation. The day was hot and unbearably humid, so the adults decided on a refreshing treat for the kids. I didn't go into the deeper water. Instead, I watched with longing as John, frolicked with our cousins, splashing, and diving into the lake's depths. I leaned back and took in the pond's cool transparency and crystal- clear water. Ojo de Agua, a natural wonder formed from a merger of rain, fresh water, and saline seawater, was unlike Galveston's water from the Gulf of Mexico, cloudy from the sand and debris and warm, like bathwater.

Our cousins of our age, ten to thirteen years old, looked to be having so much fun. I, too, wanted to be in the ruckus, but I held back because I wasn't comfortable near water. I grew up on an island, but the orthopedic doctors sheathed both legs in casts every summer to keep my feet from returning to their clubbed positions. The doctor probably believed he was considerate to plaster my legs during the summer break. He told Mama that navigating crutches in the school room and play yard was too physically demanding I could slip or fall down the stairs. It probably never occurred to him, or my mother, for that matter, that summer casts prevented summer activities like learning how to swim. Today, at least, I didn't have to manage the casts. Mama told the doctor about our trip, and he delayed it until our return. My mother and aunts kept me company, entertaining me with conversation. I remained aloof.

"Wake up!" Someone was shaking me. "Querida!"

I sat up in bed, confused, and rubbed my eyes.

"¿Eh, eh, qué pasó?" I blinked, and my brain adjusted to the present. Auntie stood beside the bed, fully dressed and ready for the day. Auntie's account of Ojo de Agua must have triggered memories of family vacations at that spot.

Auntie looked puzzled. "You were talking in your sleep. Something in Spanish."

"Oh," I explained, rubbing my face, yawning, and stretching out my arms, "That means I've acclimated to Mexico. I go to bed thinking in English and wake up speaking in Spanish."

"You'll never regret being bilingual," she gave my legs a playful slap. "Get ready; we're going to church. Tila would never forgive me if I didn't take you to Sunday mass."

I rolled my eyes. As far as I knew, Auntie had never gone to church and now wanted to take me to a service.

"Auntie, I went to Mass every day at the college chapel, even on weekends. Missing one Sunday won't matter."

Now Auntie rolled her eyes.

"Well-behaved women have no fun!" she shook her index finger, referring to my churchly devotions. I shrugged and didn't respond—I was a devoted practicing Catholic.

We attended a solemn high Mass at 10 o'clock, during which a profusion of incense permeated the building. The congregation filled the pews, and although Mass was conventional and ritualistic, people walked around the massive church during the service like they were tourists. We sat in the back, and instead of following the prayers in

Spanish, something I was unaccustomed to hearing, I observed all the goings-on. I didn't dare behave in such a casual manner during Mass. I thought back to one service when I was ten years old during a family visit to Sabinas Hidalgo with my parents, and the congregants did the same as what was happening here. I remember being confused about what I perceived as a lack of respect for the service. I was taught that the Gospel reading was the Divine Liturgy. I saw a mother holding her child, pointing to the statues next to the vestibule speaking in her daughter's ear. Then, another woman rose when the priest stood before the congregation for the sermon. She genuflected and crossed over to a pew to whisper to another woman. Then both women walked to the front of the church to light a candle as both knelt in prayer. The casual manner of mass in Mexico would never have been allowed at home.

We exited through a pink quarry Corinthian column, a copy of Roman architecture. On the way, we stopped in front of a magnificent marble Carrara shrine of the Virgin Mary situated on a pedestal. We marveled over the richly decorated altars depicting Jesus and the apostles, murals showing the majesty of God and His angels, and easel paintings of unfamiliar saints scattered throughout the massive church.

The day was breezy, and the air was fresh. Auntie and I walked less than a mile to the boardwalk. There, eclectic shops promoted well- known fashion icons rather than the typical Mexican souvenirs of clay pottery, paper mâché dolls, and paper-crafted flowers used in many Mexican venues. We came across a kiosk selling cassettes, and we both looked for an artist we liked. I searched for a song from last night, and the salesman showed me a Los Tigres del Norte cassette; Auntie picked the Best of Vicente Fernandez. We wanted a quick breakfast, and Auntie suggested we stop and pick up a meal to take to our hotel room.

"Let's go to the beach today," Auntie said. "I don't feel like being around people."

With schools shutting down for the summer, Tampico appeared to be a favorite destination. Sightseers flooded the sidewalk on our way back to the hotel.

We found a café, went inside, and ordered a take-out meal. At the hotel, we changed from our church clothes and sat at the tiny table in our room to eat. Afterward, we tidied up, put away our night clothes, and discarded the food wrappings. Auntie set the trash canister outside our door.

"We don't want the maids thinking we're vulgar and coarse women," she explained.

When heading for the car, Auntie first stopped at the front desk and inquired about the closest travel to the beach; the concierge recommended Las Escolleras, a 10 km drive.

The beach was alive; every food booth, restaurant, and large souvenir stand competed with loud music to entice tourists. At the pier's entrance, there were bicycles to rent. We favored a leisurely walk down the long promenade. Some local fishermen passed us with their catch of the day, holding to their sides what looked like catfish. In the distance, further out in the ocean, barges and tanker ships anchored in deeper waters. This reminded me of what my mother said: ships no longer docked near piers after the 1947 Texas City Disaster. I wondered if that was true at every destination where ships brought cargo to port. The day was clear, and we looked along the sandy beach where thatched-roofed cabanas shielded bathers from the sun.

I could tell Auntie was melancholy as we headed slowly toward the mile- long jetty. I thought about discussing something different from the story of Narciso and Guadalupe, my newly discovered Texas land baron kin.

"Were you living in Texas during the Disaster?"

"No, thank God," she turned to look at me. "The thought of my baby brother's brutal death was too much. That explosion created nothing but misery for Texas City; it was horrible."

The disaster occurred a year before I was born but remained a topic of conversation at family gatherings. My uncle Alex and my grandfather were longshoremen, part of the crew hired to load the ship with fertilizer headed for Europe. Both sat on the dock, awaiting orders to return to the vessel as firemen battled to contain the fire. Then the ship exploded. Alex, the youngest Canales sibling, was first hit by flying shrapnel on his chest, and, as he rolled over in agony, he was again hit on his back—the blow that killed him. Grandfather was gravely injured but lived for a several hours. An acquaintance stayed by his side and told Grandfather's children his last words. I waited to see if Auntie would continue.

"The only good thing that came from that explosion is that el Hijo del Diablo suffered before he died." I had difficulty getting used to Auntie calling her stepfather, my grandfather, son of the devil.

I shuddered at the thought. Grandfather had watched Alex's death, and, at that moment, he, too, wanted to die. As he sat beside Alex, my grandfather's arm and one leg had been amputated by flying missiles of debris from the 2300-ton vessel. When placed on a gurney for the hospital, emergency workers tried to insert a needle to give him whole blood. Grandfather told the emergency worker who wanted to provide him with blood to give it to someone else. He bled to death before receiving any surgical intervention.

"He preferred that someone younger get the blood they tried to give him," I repeated what Mama had heard.

She turned to me with a sad expression, then looked away.

"You know I've always hated my stepfather, don't you?" I nodded yes.

"I was only two when he married my mother, who was three months pregnant with my brother, Fortino. He told her that he would accept the baby as his own and for me to go by his last name," Auntie continued. "He didn't adopt me; when my brother was born six months later, the midwife assumed him the legitimate son of José and Lucia Canales. I was so young, I'd forgotten what my real father looked like, but I watched el Hijo del Diablo closely and hated him for abusing my mother for no reason."

"Is that why you want your baptismal certificate?" I asked softly.

"Just once; I want to see my birth father's name on something official," she responded. "My birth certificate looks like a letter. People I don't even know scribbled their names, attesting to the date and time of my birth, but not those of my parents. Why is that? I want to find out."

Auntie's story of the circumstances surrounding her birth were not unusual, and she usually appeared indifferent whenever I listened to my aunts' conversations about their mother, Lucia. While still a teenager, Lucia worked in the home of a doctor who'd left his family in Ireland. Lucia and the doctor fell in love, and in 1898, they escaped the gossip of Runge, Texas, for a new life in Tampico, Mexico. He opened a medical practice there and often traveled to the backwoods to care for patients.

"My Grandfather wasn't a good father?" I pushed for more information.

She turned to look at me—stone-faced.

"He was monstrous! He always beat Lucia, and he didn't need a reason. He'd be gone for months and wouldn't send her money. She had all these kids to feed. What could she do?

"Mama said that Grandmother worked picking cotton and ran a boarding house," I added.

"Yes! That's how she made ends meet. But she would pay the price whenever he was home because he couldn't stand for her not to need him."

I'd never heard this side of the story about my grandparents' relationship.

"Remember, Querida, I'm the oldest and thirteen years older than your mom. I went through all those babies and places he'd move us to because he wanted her pregnant and dependent on him. That's why my brothers and sisters were born in so many different towns."

Grandmother bore eleven babies, including Auntie and her brother Fortino. She conceived nine with my Grandfather, two of whom died in infancy.

Musicians on the beach played loud music, and, for a long time, we sat quietly on a massive boulder near the water. I took this moment to change the subject.

"I had fun last night."

She smiled, "Yes, that was fun—festive music and a lively crowd!" "You didn't like those young men, right?"

"No," she said emphatically, "they were cabrónes—scoundrels that were up to no good. I saw how they looked at you."

During high school, I was ignored by the young men from the boys' Catholic school. I certainly wouldn't recognize "how they looked at you" glances from these young men. I blamed my birth defect, then a vicious bout with acne. Being invisible to boys made me feel like a freak, and I thought myself unattractive. I chose an all-girls Catholic college so I wouldn't feel self-conscious about my appearance. However, in college, I was introduced to men from the local Catholic men's college and the military bases, and before long, I began dating. It was during these weekly activities that I began to gain the confidence I lacked in high school.

"You've been the best and most fun-est chaperone," I teased.

"Parents must safeguard their young daughters," she said earnestly, "cabrónes are out there looking to take advantage. You have to be careful whom to trust."

Was now the time to tell her about the disturbing incident that occurred during the first semester? I decided it was now or never.

"Did Mama ever tell you what happened to me at school?" "No!" she quickly answered, looking at me anxiously.

We sat on a boulder by the water, far away from passersby. I took a deep breath of the ocean breeze. My senses zeroed in on the persistent cawing of seagulls; the waves splashed against the jetty, attempting to douse our legs.

"I got sick the fall of first semester," I began. "At first, I thought I had a cold, congestion, sneezing, and a sore throat. But then it became bronchitis, laryngitis with a high fever. Sister Frances, the dorm mother, checked on me every day. One evening, she took my temperature and said she was sending me to the emergency room. 'It might be

103

pneumonia,' she told me."

Auntie listened intently.

"Sister helped me to change from pajamas. I was groggy and off-balance. She called on two seniors to drive me to the hospital as they were the only ones allowed to have cars on campus. When we got there, a nurse placed me in a room, took my temperature, and had me change into a hospital gown."

Patiently, Auntie waited for me to continue.

"When the doctor came in, an intern, I remember the nurse gave him the details of my symptoms. He told her to remove my underwear and leave the room, which she did."

Auntie's eyes widened in horror. "Did he molest you?"

"I don't know what to call the... the examination. This doctor...he inserted his fingers into my rectum and, with his other hand, pressed all over my bare stomach. Then, he stood up abruptly, he loudly said, "You have an enlarged uterus! Why do you have an enlarged uterus?" The nurse had come back in.

"What was he talking about? Did the nurse do anything?" Auntie was visibly disturbed. She took both my hands and squeezed them.

"No, he left to talk to my companions in the waiting room, and she helped me get dressed. Neither of us talked. I was embarrassed and bewildered and so confused. I didn't understand what my uterus had to do with pneumonia."

Auntie stood up and walked behind me. I turned to look at her. She was upset, and I asked myself if confiding in her had been a mistake.

"Your mother talked to you about these things, you know, about men, didn't she?"

"Not details like this. Mama always said I could tell her anything. When I was in the hospital after the corrective surgery for my clubbed feet, an acquaintance, who was dating one of my cousins, began to visit and bring me presents."

"What kinds of presents?" Auntie asked suspiciously.

"Candy, teen magazines, Kleenex, nothing outrageous—stuff that a fifteen-year-old might like. He was so much older than me by at least twenty years. Conversations were an effort because he only spoke Spanish, and I was in so much pain recovering from the bone reconstruction. He would sit and stare at me without talking. After about thirty minutes, he would politely say goodbye, nod his head, and leave. That entire summer in the hospital, I was confined to a bed with casts up to my hips. I told Mama I was extremely uncomfortable whenever he came."

"What did Tila say?"

"She said she'd take care of it." "And…?"

"She must have because he never came to see me again."

"And that's why mamas need to believe in their daughters! Good for Tila!"

We sat a moment in silence. I was relieved to tell the story without any misunderstandings.

"What else?" Auntie somehow sensed there was more.

"I was released with antibiotics, cough syrup, and what the doctor called antihistamine tablets. He told my companions I most likely had a severe allergic reaction to the mountain cedar trees whose spores spread all over San Antonio during the late fall."

"That's it? He didn't explain his examination?" Auntie's astonishment showed.

"I never had allergies in Galveston. I didn't even know what allergy meant."

"Did you say anything to anyone?" Auntie gently asked.

"The girls who drove me talked about their conversation with the doctor, so I asked them if he told them about the unexpected examination. They were shocked and began questioning me for answers I didn't have. I still don't know what prompted the doctor to examine me for something other than possible pneumonia."

"Did Sister come to talk to you? She should have." "No, nothing more was ever said."

"So, nobody acknowledged what happened?" Auntie frowned.

I sighed. "I wrote a letter to a high school friend who was a freshman at a Houston university, and I suppose I explained myself all wrong. I don't know what I was looking for, but I wanted someone to say it was wrong."

"Did she understand?"

"If she did, she told her mother, I don't know what. Her mother, in turn, relayed a sordid account to Mama about daughters having too much freedom and allowing boys to take liberties. What she said to my mother was horrible, and I still feel humiliated."

"Did Tila respond? Did she believe the woman?"

"No! She told me to finish a degree and follow a career outside of Galveston. Then I wouldn't have to live in a town filled with people who were gossipers and narrow-minded."

"So Tila's saying is true, 'women are harder on women…'" Auntie didn't finish.

I repeated my mother's phrase, "Men are harder on women than on men, but women are hardest on women than on men."

We sat quietly for several minutes. Without warning, she jumped up and grabbed my hand.

"Let's get Margaritas! I saw musicians going inside a bar. We're not going to stop having fun!"

Auntie was the perfect confidant, and relief doused my anxiety. I had never had an alcoholic drink. My nineteenth birthday wasn't until July, two months away, but Auntie had no problem ordering us Margaritas, taco chips, and guacamole.

"This is my first drink," I said.

"This is Mexico," Auntie replied gleefully, and we both raised our glasses in a toast to commemorate the occasion.

"Margaritas are wonderful!" I said, slurping through a straw.

"Mother's milk," Auntie agreed.

★

In the dark, during that stillness before conscious thoughts dim, the instant before sleep overtakes, Auntie, turned to her side, faced me, and whispered,

"You did nothing wrong, Querida; always remember that."

Chapter 8

EL AGOSTADERO DE TEJAS

Monday morning, Auntie and I woke early and languished in our beds.

"I can't believe only last Thursday you picked me up for this trip," I wistfully said.

She yawned loudly, stretching her arms and legs tautly. "Let's order breakfast in bed," she announced.

My eyes widened, "Wow, are you serious?"

She laughed and picked up the telephone, holding it to the crook of her neck, "I want time to tell you what Narciso did in the 1790s to certify his land. Besides, we deserve a leisurely day, and I still have to call the church for permission to look for my baptismal records.

Breakfast in bed, what a luxury, I thought. I finger-fluffed my hair and straightened my pillow in wait for Auntie's always fascinating tales of Narcisco.

★

In 1792, While living in his grandfather's hacienda in Nuevo Leon, Mexico, Narciso received a Royal proclamation from King Charles IV decreeing him 600,000 acres of land called El Agostadero (The Pasture) de San Juan de Carricitos. This decree, the most oversized Tejas parcel ever granted to a Spaniard, left Narciso excited and proud as he made his way to begin the applications for possession and occupation of the land. He must ready a community of followers to an unknown wilderness 87 kilometers from this established homeland.

First, he needed to record the order from the King of Spain. Narciso boastfully addressed the commissioned officer, who marveled at the land size while certifying this impressive official document bearing the Royal Crest. Next, Narciso stopped at the mayor's office, Don Lucas Canales Benavides, impressed as well, and who eagerly accompanied him to the other governmental agencies.

Narciso was a celebrity; the town's officials wanted him as their compadre.

"I'm happy to assist you, Narciso. First, make the travel arrangements to inspect the land, and a survey to set the land boundaries are in order," said Don Benavides.

"Sure, I expected that," Narciso mumbled.

Don Benavides nodded enthusiastically, "Then, you must contract appraisers and recruit witnesses to survey. They will be part of the expedition as well as myself." He bowed slightly.

Narciso felt his stomach tighten. Does the mayor know the process? "Of course, you must be familiar with the details, right? What else?"

"Um, yes, of course, although it's been a few years." He hastily concluded, "You must also meet with the adjacent landowners."

"That's going to take months," Narciso responded. "The landowners are scattered for miles in all directions. Can anyone else go as my representative?"

Don Benavides nodded his head up and down, "Why me, of course." He handed Narciso one more document. Narciso stared at it, thinking it was another long-drawn-out hurdle.

He read it out loud. "After issuing all the proceedings, post for three weeks for the public to review," Narciso sighed loudly, "Anything else?" he asked the mayor.

"After that, Narciso, the land is yours and ready for possession." The mayor smiled, and the men shook hands.

Narciso could not contain his joy. He examined the documents.

Although a massive undertaking, the time had arrived for this day. He couldn't wait to see Guadalupe still living at her parent's hacienda and having his babies without the benefit of marriage. He rushed to see her that night.

"I was right about the Land Grant bringing good fortune," Narciso reminded Guadalupe and her parents. She had given him another son, Blas. "Having sons proves that we are blessed. We'll have heirs to maintain this vast parcel," he briefed Guadalupe's skeptical parents, who were more interested in the Church's permission to marry.

As luck would have it, the dispensation arrived before Narciso left to survey. He and his first cousin, Guadalupe, were now free to marry in the Catholic Church. "We'll settle San Juan de Carricitos as husband and wife," he declared, "but for now, you and the children must come to live with me at La Hacienda De Los Cavazos."

They arranged an intimate wedding with only their immediate families on July 6, 1793, at her parent's hacienda in Montemorelos. During the celebratory dinner, Narciso stood and raised his glass.

"I believe that God bestowed all my blessings." Guadalupe smiled warmly at Narciso. "And, deep in my heart, I will never forget Maria Ignacia, the mother of my older children." Maria de los Santos, Francisca, and Manuel raised their glasses in unison; thirteen-year-old Ignacia bowed to hide oncoming tears.

"I renew my vow to build a chapel in Maria Ignacia's memory," Narciso continued, "and for her deep devotion to the Church."

★

Later that year, Narciso completed the preliminary requirements. He readied a team for the handover required by Spanish law, a ritual necessary to transfer the property from the Crown to Narciso. For months, his closest friend, Raúl, made ready several vaqueros, including a cook and three wagons led by mules with enough supplies and provisions for the twenty-one-day expedition.

Excitement permeated the hacienda compound as the family waited for the officials accompanying Narciso.

One morning, while Guadalupe and Narciso were having breakfast on the veranda, a servant girl placed a tray on the table with several calling cards. Narciso looked at them, threw the cards back onto the tray, and rushed to the receiving room. Guadalupe hurried behind him. The emissaries had arrived. The mayor and two others sat restlessly, tapestry travel bags at their feet. The guests stood and bowed politely with hands extended in greeting.

"Don Benavides," Narciso excitedly took his hand and shook it. "Of course, Mayor, welcome!"

The mayor extended his arm toward the two gentlemen at his side.

"I present my brother-in-law, the attorney, Señor Cristobal Salinas Canales, and Señor Pedro Jesús Flores, a court reporter. Señor Canales will describe the land's dividing lines, and Señor Flores will record the borderlines with drawings."

Guadalupe smiled as she closed the door to the receiving room, where the men remained for most of the day. With Ignacia, her stepdaughter, and two servant girls, she began preparing a celebratory meal for the family and guests. Three-year-old Jorge, two-year-old-Clara, and one-year-old Blas noisily played with their toys as their mother joyfully instructed and prepared a banquet.

"We're cooking a feast to invoke God's blessing for a successful journey," she told the young women cheerfully.

The dinner guests and hosts dined in an atmosphere of animated and boisterous conversations. They spoke of the wild open Tejas land, the acres, and acres of barren countryside, and the ferocious Indians hiding in the thicket. Guadalupe constantly smiled and giggled at Narciso's talk of taming the wild frontier. Together, they would do whatever it took to build a splendid community and a home for their growing family. Their eyes met. The smiling couple announced their latest news;

Guadalupe was once again pregnant.

The following day, as he came from the stable leading Haro, Narciso saw a large crowd assembled and waved his hat. They had arrived at La Hacienda de Los Cavazos to commemorate Narciso's family and to wish him and the team safe travels. People outside the community wanted to be part of applauding Narciso's good fortune.

San Juan de Carricitos was 205 kilometers from La Hacienda, a journey of two and a half days. The vaqueros traveling with Narciso nicknamed the caravan Los Peregrinos, the Pilgrims. It consisted of eight men, including Narciso and the emissaries, who rode horseback or in one of the three wagons.

Narciso waved a leather, flat-crowned, wide-brimmed sombrero and announced to the party, "For God, the King, and Country. This journey is God's will!" The crowd roared in approval.

The clothes and boots Narciso and the vaqueros sported were of rugged, durable denim and leather fabrics to protect their bodies from bushes of thorns and thistles. He feared for his guests whose wardrobes lacked the durability for wilderness terrain.

"Remember what we talked about last night," he told the guests, "the journey takes twenty-two hours to get there. We still don't know how long we'll need to survey."

The emissaries nodded. "We're ready," they responded in unison.

"And the terrain is wild. We'll be traveling through virgin territory," Narciso hesitated and stared at the men.

They nodded yes again. "We're well aware that it's going to be an untamed wilderness," Señor Canales assured Narciso, "I've done this before."

Narciso raised his eyebrows. He then turned to face Guadalupe and blew her a kiss. With the caravan ready to advance, he mounted Haro and waved his hat again.

"Let the journey begin!" he shouted.

The compound erupted in waving handkerchiefs and scarves. Friends, neighbors, and servants reached for each other for hugs while shouting and whooping. Narciso spotted his sisters and sisters-in- law smiling on the porch of the main hacienda, waving lace handkerchiefs. Holding Blas in her arms, Guadalupe and Ignacia stood on the porch smiling broadly. Jorge and Clara joined in the merriment and happily toddled behind the other children chasing after the caravan. For Narciso and Guadalupe, this was their moment, and both were united in the dream. He turned for another look at Guadalupe, and she blew him a kiss.

★

Los Peregrinos were now ten weeks into tracking and record-keeping. They followed the original landmarks recorded in 1747 by José de Escandón, the colonizer of Texas. Conspicuous objects that marked a locality were charted and mapped. Two men in Narciso's caravan would scout ahead to the area on the map while two others trailed behind at a distance. The court reporter, Pedro, was a slight, nervous man whose delicate hands were quick as a whip when he put pen to paper and made drawings of the landscape, marking the property's boundaries. The vaquero accompanying Pedro carried medallions with the Cavazos coat-of-arms to mark the spots that didn't appear on the original map but exhibited a distinctive trademark, such as a stream or an ancient oak tree. Once Pedro sketched the landscape, the witnesses, Narciso's brothers, Nazario and Francisco, signed the page.

At each north, south, east, and west boundary, Narciso had to perform the ritual of Spanish law requiring that he and only he blend a mixture of collected grass, broken twigs, handfuls of dirt, and water his hands scooped. He then deposited this composition on the ground—an offering comprising the precious minerals from his land. He repeated this ritual again and again until the last boundary.

In the distance, Narciso thought he saw a lone figure on a horse at an out-of-the-way spot, so he moved to shield his eyes from the sun's rays as he peered in the direction of the vision. It had disappeared, but from then on, Narciso couldn't shake the feeling of being watched.

The emissaries struggled with the daily demands; the severe and coarse terrain, the dry and semi-arid soil Narciso scratched with his nails and dug with his hands, the brutally humid climate, and the eternal sunshine that required frequent stops for water for themselves, and the animals. Los Peregrinos unmounted their horses and guided them on foot through acres and acres of overgrown, wild, dense grasslands toward the next available water source. At times, a grass path swayed like a waving flag as a snake slithered unseen. The faces of the emissaries would turn ashen as they wiped clammy hands on their clothing, momentarily stopping to listen for a rattle. The scamper of a small animal hiding in the dense grass would elicit a gasp from the traveler unaccustomed to the sights and sounds of the wilderness. Occasionally they encountered a family of deer. None of the men escaped the blisters, redness, itching, and irritation from the relentless bites of insects and mosquitoes. The vaqueros continually burned bunches of sweetgrass and sage to repel the insects.

Narciso persisted with unwavering vigor. He maintained high spirits and appeared in a perpetual state of exhilaration. At night, around the campfire, head relaxed on his saddle, he'd study the ledger documenting their progress.

"Let me show you where the next water source will be," he would say, raising the map and locating the spot. "This one is where I'll dig wells for irrigation. And this one," he sat up and pointed a finger on the map, "the well that Escandón had dug and built…that is where I'll build the hacienda so water will be convenient to access."

He looked at Pedro, the scribe lying still in his bedroll. Narciso slapped his leg and handed him a slip of paper. "Record the coordinates for this water source we came across today!"

Pedro sat up and reached for the ledger.

Narciso continued, "The land is part of the drainage basins of the Rio Grande and Pecos Rivers. Look at the map." He paused, the others were asleep, and one was snoring loudly.

Narciso snickered. "Go ahead, Pedro, go to sleep. Tomorrow we'll begin to chronicle more of this massive land." He smiled as he crawled into his bedroll. But his senses were on the alert; someone was watching.

★

Narciso arrived home late in the evening. Relieved to have him safely at home, Guadalupe drew him a hot bath and sat close by. "I felt like an intruder," he told her. " I could feel the eyes of those who roam the land following me whenever I performed the required ritual."

He looked at Guadalupe, who shook her head. "You're not taking their land, Narciso, their people live elsewhere. That's why Spain gave you that area—a no man's land, remember?" "They may live elsewhere," he replied, "but we are the intruder." That night, they held each other close, content, and happy in each other's embrace."

The next morning, Narciso sat against the bed's headboard and laughed loudly, "The King of Spain granted me almost 79 leagues.4 of land, the largest one ever given to a Spanish subject!" He kissed Guadalupe on her head. "I've dreamed of this for all my life, and now I have enough leagues on which to build a legacy," Narciso turned his face upward and let out a loud whoop.

In a long muslin dressing gown with lace ruffles, Guadalupe smiled and rolled over on her side. She adjusted her back on the pillows. She hollered, sat up, and blew out a deep breath. "This child must be a boy; he's constantly kicking."

Narciso went over to her side and knelt by the bed. He placed his hand gently on her belly. "We'll need all the hombres we can get to build this settlement," he grinned.

He then stood straight in military posture, "I see myself as the leader of a grand entrada," he said to Guadalupe. "I now know how Oñate felt when he led the exhibition into New Mexico," he sat on the bed's edge and pulled on his trousers.

Guadalupe sat up from her pillows, brows furrowed, "So you think moving to this land is the same as Oñate's exploration?" The Cavazos descended from Juan de Oñate, a historical figure even then—the conquistador who founded New Mexico for the Spanish crown.

"Of course," Narciso turned to face her. "This wilderness is untouched and unsettled. We…I am a master architect. And you, mi Cariña, you're the Doña of El Agostadero. We can even start a town and name it Guadalupe."

She burst into laughter; her eyes sparkled in glee over this remarkable opportunity and her handsome, clever husband.

"I have to leave with the group of men for several weeks, mi Cariña." Narciso knelt facing her. There's much to be done before this baby comes if we're resettling our family and others." He placed his hand again on her belly. Guadalupe smiled and nodded, her hand over his.

★

Guadalupe remained at the hacienda in Mexico while Narciso and his crew left to fulfill the first phase of his requirement, the main house in Tejas. The place he would eventually build would be a modest version of the one in Nuevo Leon, but for now, he had to make the main house structure comply with the terms of occupation.

"In time, I can make it as big as La Hacienda De Los Cavazos," Narciso told himself. "Mi Cariña will like that."

Narciso was happier than he'd ever been. Every detail was falling into place. He even delineated the cultivated land parcels he would give to his children, family members, and those devoted followers fulfilling the dreams of land ownership in Tejas.

"All my children will have land to build for future generations. After the little ones are grown, the children and their families will remain close to Cariña and me." He enjoyed romanticizing their old age together.

Throughout the compound, Narciso, alongside Raúl and the men, constructed one and two-room jacales[5] for the loyal followers and their families. They finalized the sheds and outbuildings to house the livestock. They made enclosures for the chickens and protective pens for farrowing sows and cows. They even cleared an area for a kitchen garden.

In 1793, a year after receiving the decree granting him land, Narciso moved his family and followers to El Agostadero de San Juan de

Carricitos. Guadalupe, strong enough to travel with their newest baby, a three-month-old girl they named Teresa, saw that this latest addition enjoyed being among her siblings, Jorge, now three; Clara, two, and Blas, one.

The caravan included Narciso's settlers and their families. They brought 400 horses, 1600 mules, 3000 mares, and 3000 cattle. The cattle, brought from Spain to Mexico in 1521, was a breed known for its characteristic horns and later to be known as the Texas Longhorns. The new open field, clear of fencing and barriers, allowed the branded cattle to roam freely and to scatter.

Chapter 9

EL TEMPLO DE LA IMMACULATA CONCEPCIÓN

Our lazy morning in bed was just what we needed. I combined our trays with the dirty breakfast dishes. "Just leave it outside the door," Auntie told me, "a maid will take care of it." She kept laying dresses across her bed. My mind whirled in many directions, thinking of my ancestor Narciso's emotional and physical ups and downs with his young family, Ignacia, her mother's loyal servants, and the followers who moved with him to settle in unknown territory.

"Remember Querida," Auntie reminded me as she lifted an orange floral print with white accents on the collar, sleeves, and pockets. "This one," she said under her breath. She looked up and continued, "Narciso and Guadalupe had to pave the way with excitement and optimism. Otherwise, who would want to join them? They both had to have been very charismatic for his followers to take this chance."

I went to the closet to pick out a dress, too, a breezy sleeveless A-line. "It would be like someone today saying, 'Hey, we're going into the Amazon jungle where we'll assemble huts and live there permanently. Forget the perks of living in the hacienda. You'll have to raid the landscape for the materials you'll need to build a home suited to your family.'"

Auntie laughed, "We wouldn't be here if Narciso stayed safely in Mexico. What if the dispensation to marry Guadalupe hadn't come through?

Think about this," she stopped, "what kind of a man would Narciso have become with unfulfilled dreams? What would have become of Guadalupe and her children? We may never have been born."

Auntie's points had never occurred to me.

"Narciso had to build an entire community from the ground up," Auntie began again, "those who joined him had a lot of confidence in his leadership to follow him. He promised them land, but Narciso had to demonstrate they would be successful."

I sat on my bed and hugged my knees. "The people who joined Narcisco and Guadalupe had to have a lot of courage, too."

"I need the perfect dress," Auntie distracted me by holding up the dress for my approval. "I want the Padre to know I'm from a respectable family. I may be illegitimate, but that doesn't brand me as undeserving."

I never knew how to talk about Auntie's illegitimacy with her, my mother, or anyone else. Yes, I knew my grandmother Lucia had run away at sixteen with her lover and had gotten pregnant with Auntie, but no one in the family acted as if it was a big deal. Was it not? I'd sit on our front porch and watch the neighborhood during those inactive periods when my legs were in casts. I noticed the neighbor women gathered in a tight circle, whispering, and shooting long glowering glances whenever a neighbor girl showed affection with a boy, such as cuddling too close, kissing in public, or sliding into a car with him close to nightfall.

And it wasn't just my neighborhood that had dubious standards. This past year at the dorm, a small-town, Catholic school-educated girl who got pregnant was dismissed but still allowed to attend classes. She and I had a similar upbringing; wildflowers in high school where no one paid attention, but once in San Antonio, we turned heads at college social events. We both worked part-time jobs in the cafeteria. She fell in love early in the dating game. However, she could no longer work on campus when she got pregnant. Attending classes was acceptable as long as she did not associate with dorm classmates. I would meet her off-campus to memorize anatomy for our biology class. I had difficulty figuring out a moral code aimed only at girls.

As a teenager, I always heard that if a girl engaged in unmarried relations, it was a dirty and evil act. However, by pronouncing the vows of marriage in front of a priest, the sex act became the means for procreation and therefore beautiful. The consequence of illicit mating was the illegitimate child, an infant who was a gift from God. Talk about confusing! Furthermore, this classmate's isolation only added to her mystique. I steered the conversation to my grandfather, whom I always saw as my grandmother's champion.

After all, he married Grandmother knowing she was pregnant with a second child by her lover.

"But Grandfather José adopted you, right?" I said in a somewhat defensive tone. "You are a Canales."

"I'm above all a Cavazos because of Mama Lucia," she said firmly. "I want to see my birth father's signature on the baptismal certificate. Besides," she continued, "that Cabrón was never my father." My grandfather held no redeeming qualities in Auntie's eyes.

I understood, embraced by a wave of sympathy. Auntie wanted proof of her parent's love for each other and her. She hated my grandfather, describing him as a monster. He was abusive and irresponsible toward his growing family, and Auntie witnessed the consequences.

Since I never got to know my grandparents, I believed her. I didn't pursue the conversation any further.

We arrived at the church rectory, and Auntie told the receptionist the reason for our visit. The woman introduced herself and ushered us into the sitting room. "Un momento. Wait a moment," she said politely and left the room.

A few minutes later, a tall, thin man in a cassock with alabaster hair and the bluest eyes entered the room.

"Soy, Padre Simón Montoya," smiling, he took Auntie's hand and looked straight into her eyes. "a su servicio. I'm Father Simon Montoya at your service."

"Sra. Eloisa Cavazos Diaz," Auntie returned the greeting and turned to me, "y mi sobrina, Barbara Esquivel."

Padre took my hand and gave me a gentle shake. He gestured for us to sit, and Auntie told him we had traveled from Texas.

"¿Habla Ingles? Padre asked, "Porque siempre estoy buscando una oportunidad para practicar. Do you speak English because I'm always looking for an opportunity to practice?"

"Sí, ah, yes," Auntie replied and turned to look at me. I nodded in appreciation. Spanish was my first language, which we always spoke at home. I never thought it unusual because we also spoke Spanish when traveling to Mexico. When my brother and I started school, Mama insisted we attend Catholic schools. Daddy demanded if he was going to pay for an education, we would attend a predominately Anglo one, so we'd learn to speak English correctly. We attended St. Patrick's instead of Our Lady of Guadalupe, and I'd translate for Daddy when Mama was unavailable for a parent session.

Mama saved all our report cards, and I made a lot of Cs in first grade. However, after that, I blossomed academically. Daddy died when John and I were in the ninth and eighth grades. It was then that we began to speak only English. Without practice, my Spanish vocabulary shrunk. I'd lose track of the conversation when the Spanish dialogue took on a more sophisticated phraseology.

"Padre Montoya, I'm looking for my baptismal certificate." Auntie began. "I was born in Tampico, Mexico, on March 19, 1899. My parents weren't married, and my father died when I was two-and-a-half. If I was baptized, I'm certain this is the place."

"Call me Padre Simón," he said, looking first to Auntie, then me.

"Padre Simón," Auntie responded immediately, "my mother ensured baptisms for all eight of my brothers and sisters in Texas. I am the first-born."

"Ah yes, first-born children are held, dear. The records are all here from the beginning," the Padre said, "we will certainly try to locate them."

"Today?" Auntie asked.

Padre Simón slapped his hands on his lap and stood. "We will try, but first, I have to call our sexton, Dario. He took the time to organize the records and is very protective. Excuse me, and I'll check to see if he can join us." He left the room.

Auntie was delighted and, with shining eyes, whispered, "Isn't he gorgeous?"

"I suppose," I responded. Educated in Catholic institutions my entire life, half of them in all girl's schools, I saw priests as unsexed ecclesiastics. I never knew of one whom I thought of as attractive.

Padre Simón told us to return in an hour or so, and Dario would help to locate the records.

We stepped out into the street, and Auntie reminded me of her desire to visit the Huasteca Museum.

"The museum has no entrance fee, and all the exhibits are on the first floor. It's small, and we can probably see the collection in about an hour."

We walked for a brisk five minutes. When we entered the building, the attendant handed us pamphlets in both English and Spanish describing the art pieces.

"What got you interested in the Huasteca?" I asked Auntie, "I've never heard of them."

"Oh, you'd better brush up on history. It's an ancient civilization from the 10th century BC," Auntie responded. "Did you think that the Spaniards were the first people in Mexico?"

I'd never thought about it. My history lessons were never about the Spaniards or the native tribes. "But how did you first hear about them?" I insisted. Everything—the name, the culture, the artifacts—was new to me. "What caught your eye about them?"

I had no cultural experience except for one in the tenth grade when our class attended the opera *Carmen* in Houston. The storyline of a wild unscrupulous Spanish gypsy was confusing to a sixteen-year-old with no romantic history. The costumes were elaborate and vibrant. I enjoyed it even though I believed the purpose of attending was to follow the French lyrics since French was a required course at Ursuline Academy. Otherwise, why did we participate?

Auntie shrugged, "I read about the museum's opening in the home newspaper. The article gave a synopsis of their history. The Aztec king, Moctezuma, and the Huasteca were bitter enemies because the Huasteca refused to pay tribute to Moctezuma. The Aztecs considered the Huasteca barbarians and unworthy of sacrifice to the Aztec gods. Later the Spaniards who came to Mexico conquered the Huasteca along with the Aztecs."

The first artifact we came across was an enormous six-foot statue made of stone. According to the pamphlet, it represented a Huasteca god/goddess with male and female features. A giant headdress symbolized the crown of a deity or a monarch. The colossal head featured a male face with a wide-opened mouth. Inside the mouth protruded a perfectly formed delicate female face. The statue's neck was slim, like a female's, and adorned with a jeweled necklace. The female neck sat atop the broad square nape of a male. The body of the statue was androgynous yet bare-breasted, indicating a female. The strong shoulders symbolized a man's strength, yet the hands at the waist were delicate and feminine. I gazed at this unusual statue for a long time.

Auntie stood beside me and smiled enthusiastically, "The Huasteca never wore clothing. The Spanish missionaries converted them to Catholicism and required them to clothe their bodies."

I stood mesmerized.

Even ancient women wore garments to display their attributes. We moved to a display where many statues represented women, and I looked at a tiny, intricately crafted one the size of my hand. This statue had an ornate braided crown with a matching braided patterned belt around her waist. She appeared to be clothed, but the garment clung, outlining her voluptuous features. I shook my head in awe.

"You think women were revered?" I asked Auntie. I thought the elaborate jewelry and accessories must have been gifts from an admirer.

Auntie nodded her head, "I don't know. However, women always had their place in the home, raising children, keeping house, cooking, you know, women's work. When the English came to America, their women accompanied the men. But the Spaniards were soldiers, all-male troops, and the women were typically a token of the spoils of war. Does that show women held in high regard"

I stared at the statues, mostly of women. It had never occurred to me that women were mistreated and abused. I took a while to respond, "I had no idea."

"You know why the Spaniards baptized the Indians and gave them Christian names?" Auntie's look was serious, and I nodded no. "Because the Catholic Spaniards couldn't engage in sexual relations with heathens."

Here was that confusing dilemma again—women, the keepers of the moral code, had no power in its enforcement. Even the priests were purveyors. Auntie kept pitching me surprises.

"Women were forced into marrying soldiers?"

Auntie raised her shoulders. "If indeed soldiers married them."

She smiled and continued, "We may have Huasteca in our genes because of one of these women.

"Wow!" That amazed me—and something different to think about. At least, this was something I understood. I always considered myself a Mexican mixed with Spanish."

Racial undertones seemed to exist in even the most proper of Mexican households. Mexicans who boasted as descendants of Europeans never recognized nor admitted that they could also possess an Indian bloodline. This was also true of my parents. While they prided themselves as descendants of royalty, they didn't admit to the possibility of a native connection in the genes. But Auntie said that the Spaniards came to the new world without women…

"Is that why some of our cousins are brown skinned?" I must have had a funny look on my face because Auntie laughed and said, "Let's head back to the church."

★

We met Dario, a short man with a limp. I looked at his feet. He wore orthopedic shoes, and the right one was elevated to correct the stance on this shorter leg.

Before my surgery, I had a distinctive limp because my right leg was a couple of inches shorter than my left. Reconstructive surgery corrected the deformity by lengthening the tendons and fusing the hindfoot. I immediately felt rapport. I still remember how good it felt with my casts removed and for the first time in three months after the surgery, both feet touched the cool tiled floor.

Dario and Auntie got on in an instant; he spoke English.

He escorted us to a small, dark, windowless room that smelled like the library on campus. He excused himself. Upon his return, Dario placed a card drawer on the table.

"The cards are alphabetized by the father's name and by the year," Dario informed us.

Auntie began to shuffle through her file. Dario brought in a drawer for me, then one for him.

"We'll start with the year. The baptisms, weddings, and funerals are recorded in large parish registries, but I've been typing the information on cards for cross-reference. What are the names?"

Auntie looked at him. I noticed her chin tremble. "I don't know how to answer," she said, "it may be under my father's name, Séamos Manus, but since my parents weren't married, maybe it's under my mother's name, Lucia Cavazos."

We spent three hours looking at card files with no luck.

"I'll bring the original registries." Dario carried a large, heavy-bound book to the table. "I have a dozen more from that period."

The script was elaborate and in Spanish, making reading difficult. We each took a book and painstakingly reviewed every name. Another three hours passed. We found nothing.

Dario closed his book, and with a pained stare looked up at Auntie. "I'm so sorry."

I felt his sincerity. Auntie smiled, "We gave it all we had, didn't we? It's not meant to be."

Dario left the room and returned with Padre.

"I'm sorry the records didn't turn up," Padre said softly, "perhaps the times were too turbulent for your parents to risk a baptism."

"Yes," Auntie agreed, "perhaps, but the times were changing during that period of relative peace in Mexico. Modern industries were taking people out of agricultural fields to work in factories. My father was a physician whose services would have been needed."

Padre Simón stared at his empty hands and again softened his response, "Lo siento," I'm sorry.

Auntie looked at Padre Simón and asked, "Can I leave a donation in memory of my parents? I never felt so gladly received in God's house." She opened her purse and pulled out her wallet.

Padre Simón bowed slightly and responded, "I will offer tomorrow's mass in their memory; thank you."

She then turned to Dario, "I mean it sincerely. What you did today was over and above your duties. Will you allow me to pay you for your services?"

I thought he was going to cry when his eyes filled with tears.

"No, Señora, no. It was my duty, and my heart breaks, that I could not bring a joyful conclusion to your search."

We headed for the hotel. I kept quiet, waiting for Auntie to start a conversation, also feeling bad that we didn't locate Auntie's certificate.

Auntie smiled, took my hand, and squeezed it. "I guess we'll have to try finding it in Texas. You up for more adventures?"

I squeezed her hand back. "Of course! I wouldn't miss it for the world!"

"Besides," she said, pulling me close, "you need to hear more of Narciso's story."

Chapter 10

DEVELOPING A LEGACY

Auntie and I strolled back to the hotel. El Temple de la Immaculata Church wasn't her baptismal site. We just sat on our beds briefly, not saying anything. Auntie then got up and pulled a suitcase from the doorless closet. She slowly began to pack.

"Tonight, we're going to have dinner by the ocean," she said cheerily. "We'll leave early in the morning to have the light of day driving back to Texas."

Auntie was putting on a happy face. She couldn't locate her baptismal certificate, and I knew she must be devastated. Still no paper trail of her father's existence, a father she barely remembered. My heart ached for her, but for me, too; I felt let down as this wonderful trip drew to a close.

"I have no regrets; she told me as if reading my mind. She neatly folded her clothes and placed them into her suitcase."

"Thank you for bringing me on this adventure, Auntie," I said softly. I got up and put my arms around her. She stopped packing and wrapped her arms around me.

"I will always remember the fun and all we shared," I told her. "This was my trip of a lifetime."

Both of us had moist eyes, but neither of us cried.

"We'll get Margaritas at supper. In Mexico, it's still legal for you to drink alcohol," she added mischievously. I would turn nineteen in July

1967, but Texas' drinking age since 1909 was twenty-one.

The following day after breakfast, Auntie finalized our check-out, and by seven o'clock, we were on the road making our way back to Texas, a six-hour drive.

"Hmm," Auntie pressed her lips together. "Once we cross the Matamoros border, we might stop along the small towns of Texas that may have been part of the Agostadero.

I got excited, "What towns?"

Auntie hesitated, "San Antonio was already there in 1899, but Lucia," she turned to look at me, "my mother was born in Runge, 60 miles from San Antonio. Maybe she baptized me in San Antonio, at the San Fernando Cathedral when she fled from Mexico." Auntie still hoped to find her baptismal certificate, and San Antonio was part of the route back to Galveston.

"Anyway," she continued, "after San Antonio, we'll stop at places that may once have been part of the Agostadero; Runge, Granite Mountain, New Braunfels, Goliad, and Lockhart."

"I'll look at the map and see how these towns chart on Narciso's land," I offered, excitedly. This trip seemed far from over.

Auntie began with the next installment of Narciso's story. "Try to imagine acres and acres of remote, unsettled fields. There were no buildings or structures. In most cases, the land was filled with undulating grassland, bushes, and trees, a rich habitat for plants, animals, and the Indians who lived off the land. The territory Narciso obtained required constructing a community from the ground up."

★

The sprawling 600,000-acre San Juan de Carricitos, el Agostadero, was prime pasture in the middle of nowhere. The closest town was the budding community of Brownsville, Texas, 48 miles away.

Brownsville, Texas, and Matamoros, Mexico, were essential cattle and trade centers, with business enterprises on both sides of the river.

When selling or trading livestock, Narciso would travel ten to twelve hours to the Rio Grande border situated at the Rio Grande River and engage in business on both sides of the border. Cattle sold at the border were shipped to either the East of the United States or to the West of Mexico.

The Revolutionary War (1765-1790) in America allowed Brownsville stable growth because the Rio Grande was the principal port for European provisions, supplying the Patriots seeking independence from England. But Narciso's land was further south from Brownsville, a vast untouched wildland and home to the Native population, the Karankawa, who migrated from the coast of the Gulf of Mexico into the Texas wilderness.

The Karankawa were not happy to see the newcomers and viewed this colonial settlement with hostility. From the beginning of European colonization, they had violent encounters with the Spanish.

Narciso and Raúl were finishing up Raúl's cabin. "The Indians returned, and this time they took five cows with their calves," he told Narciso.

Narciso turned abruptly to face him. "Maybe the cows went to graze at a better pasture. They have a wide range." He waved his arm in a circular sweep.

Raúl straightened his back and folded his arms, "No, the vaqueros and I thoroughly checked."

"Spanish soldiers began this hostility with the Karankawa," Narciso told Raúl. "They attacked and ambushed them to build the Presidio."[6]

"That was then. I'm talking about now," Raúl interjected. "We're exposed. Our center of defense is the garrison 300 miles away in San Antonio,[7] which houses eighty troops who protect their settlers and ranchers. We're facing frequent Indian menaces, Narciso, even if we don't have to fight to defend our community."

"My contract clearly states I must negotiate with the Indians," Narciso sighed; he realized the Indians saw their land dwindling and prey animals disappearing due to disrupted breeding grounds from outsiders. "I still have four years to get it done."

"Four more years?" Raúl clenched his jaw. "After they burn the buildings and begin to kill us? What if they steal our horses? What if one of them tries to take Haro?"

Narciso must negotiate with the Karankawa people who understood they were losing land.

Narciso chuckled, but not in humor, "There is no man who can ride Haro; he would toss him in an instant." He thought about the morning he found a colorful blanket, clearly Indian, covering Haro, chewing on a slow-feed hay net, neatly formed, and tied with twine.

Both men quieted. They picked up their work tools and joined the other men working on finishing Raúl's cabin. They had cleared the grass and cut the trees into logs. Narciso's cabin, the main structure, now housed his family of three adults and soon-to-be five young children. He built his house near the well Escandón, which the original colonizer of this region of Texas had built when determining Texas land borders. Narciso also planted a garden, built a barn with a stall for Haro and a couple of milk cows, and fenced it for a chicken coop.

"Has Haro ever stayed in his stall?" Raúl asked.

"No," Narciso answered, moving away from Raúl to chop branches off tree limbs while thinking. *But how did that Indian get that blanket on Haro without his creating a violent fuss?* His beautiful Andalusian horse from the Iberian Peninsula of Spain was his treasure, his twenty-first birthday gift from his grandfather. He had named him Haro after Castile's most powerful medieval family, the House of Haro, Narciso's ancestor. His flawless black coat, free of any markings, glowed satiny and shiny in the blazing sun; his mane and tail were like strands of silk. Narciso brushed and groomed him daily to maintain his European regal appearance. *If I tie him in his stall, he'll kick and bellow until he awakens and frightens the community.* Everyone knew that Haro was mulish.

The community didn't know how to mollify the Indians while taking over their terrain. Narciso had to devise a plan. He couldn't risk losing

Haro to Indian brujería; magic was the only way to lure Haro away from Narciso.

Narciso designated a parcel to each settler he promised land to, and the men and their families also required living quarters. They dug trenches for irrigation and set plots for grazing and farming. Each member receiving land had to construct an adobe shelter or a log home and assign fields for grazing and agriculture, planting beans, corn, potatoes, and sugarcane. Narciso's large one-room structure became the meeting place for the people to measure progress and dispense ideas.

"Beginning a new life from scratch is something for young people," Narciso told Raúl one day while clearing a spot for a jacala. He sighed heavily. He was now forty-two years old. "Had I known it would take ten years to acquire this land, I would have submitted my application when I turned twenty-one." Narciso stood, bent backward, and rubbed his lower back.

Raúl laughed, "We were both too busy having fun and enjoying privileges, weren't we?"

Unsmiling, Narciso nodded yes. His life in his grandfather's hacienda had been one of privilege. He could engage in labor and arduous work, which he often did, but he never had to complete a full day of manual labor, and, before now, he had no idea what continuous physical hand work entailed day in and day out.

"We must work nonstop to complete the government requirements." Narciso stretched again.

Raúl nodded in agreement as he wiped the sweat from his face. "Yep, we should have done this ten years ago."

The conditions to keep Spain from repossessing his land hung heavy on Narciso's mind. He must show growth by expanding and replenishing with new members. The town's central plaza, the public living room, was essential for gatherings, meetings, and social and political discourse, in addition to maintaining cultural continuity. He needed shops that provided goods, and a church to hold the community together. Within five years, progress must be evident when the officials come to check.

1794 was rapidly coming to an end, but he still had four years.

Narciso and his community of settlers established a town center and a clapboard general store to stock goods imported from Mexico. Initially, it only stocked necessities like dry goods, soap, candles, and farming tools bought on credit. The settlers could settle their accounts later with the harvest. In accordance with his sworn allegiance to uphold the Catholic religion and convert the Indians, he must build a church.

"We need to secure Mama's memory," fourteen-year-old Ignacia reminded her father one evening at supper. Her mother, Maria Ignacia, had died four years ago at La Hacienda. "A chapel in her honor must be built. Two families who served Mamá as her servants loved her enough to believe in you and are here at the Agostadero to serve in the community."

"I know, Ignacia," Narciso responded. "That's one of my priorities," thinking how her mother's memory was never far from her heart.

"Also include a school for the children," Ignacia added. She rose from the table and glanced from Guadalupe to Narciso, "I'll get the coffee."

The younger children scattered to the outdoor veranda when other children in the community yelled for them to play. Narciso chuckled, addressing them, "Be careful little ones—Jorge, watch your little brother and sisters." He looked at the door and rose abruptly.

Indians were known to kidnap women and children, he thought to himself. He stepped onto the veranda and saw two couples conversing close to where the children were playing. One of the men patted his hip, indicating to Narciso the lance he wore on watch. Narciso waved back.

Narciso pinched the bridge of his nose and said to Guadalupe, "Each day blends into another as this feverish work continues. I must make the church a priority." Lowering his voice, "I've never been overly religious, but now I feel God had a hand in granting us all our dreams."

"Shouldn't a church have been erected before our arrival?" Guadalupe asked. "Look at the surrounding families that acquired grants before you."

Narciso shrugged his shoulders. "Perhaps the rules didn't apply." Guadalupe continued, "Other land grants have been around since the 1770s. Why weren't they required to complete a church or chapel within five years?" She named the four notable grants surrounding San Juan de Carricitos. [8]

Narciso looked at Guadalupe. "Perhaps they have chapels; I don't know. I'm too tired to think about anything but sleep. I can build a chapel, but a church in five years?"

"How can I help?" Speaking softly, Guadalupe covered her other hand over the one he was holding. Ignacia placed a tray of coffee and bunuelos, a Mexican pastry made with flour tortillas fried in butter and sprinkled with cinnamon and sugar.

Narciso looked into Guadalupe's eyes, "Not at this time. You're pregnant and depend on Ignacia to help; he smiled at his daughter. "Besides, as the Doña, you must set aside time and your strength for religious and social activities." Ignacia leaned to kiss his cheek.

While social activities did include festivals, they primarily involved community projects in which the women gathered to plow and plant a kitchen garden, preserve quantities of vegetables and meats, and instruct the children in prayers.

The duties of this vital element to building a community fell to Guadalupe, now twenty. She had organized a party for Ignacia, who celebrated her fourteenth birthday at San Juan de Carricitos.

Guadalupe prepared a home-cooked meal of mole, a Mexican chicken dish made with a chocolate sauce and traditional beans and rice. Several músicos caseros, homespun musicians, brought guitars to excite the guests to sing and dance on the dirt floor of the temporary plaza.

"The community did enjoy the birthday party," Narciso smiled widely.

Next year we'll throw her a quinceañera.

They would send out invitations to the surrounding grantees to notify guests. The quinceañera was a coming-out party given by elite families to introduce their comit daughters to suiters to procure a marriage contract with a beau of her choosing.

The children's delighted laughs filled the open doorway. The adults quietly ate pastries and sipped coffee.

"I have to tell you something," Narciso began, and both women looked at him. Raúl and I must go tomorrow to recover a few lost cows and their calves."

Not only was day-to-day living precarious, but the women often spent days managing alone.

Guadalupe sat up straight and, with a haughty tone, said, "We're young and strong. Work consumes the lives of both the men and the women."

Narciso felt relief but was still apprehensive about leaving Guadalupe and Ignacia alone.

"Maybe you could gather the women on some quilting function or something, so you'll be together in one place," he suggested.

Guadalupe smiled, "You taught me how to shoot, and the women all keep a sharp knife in their boots. No man or beast is safe around us."

"Still," Narciso said, "I'd like for you to gather the women here at the house."

Early the following day, Raúl and four horsemen greeted Narciso.

"These vaqueros volunteered to help."

"Do we need this many men for five cows?" Narciso thought but didn't speak. "I need them here as guards." However, Narciso was relieved to see the women with their sewing baskets and their children approaching his house.

Solemnly, Guadalupe watched as Narciso placed into Haro's saddlebags a machete and other tools for cutting the rough, wooded areas. He moved beside her.

"Mi Cariña, everything I do is for our future and our children."

"I know," she sighed deeply, "you were gone three weeks a couple of months ago. I didn't know if you were alive or dead," she grasped Narciso's arms and lifted her head to make eye contact. "Keep us informed with a messenger or two. Remember, while you tackle the land and the animals, I confront the grass so tall they hide Indians and their secrets."

"They will not harm you," Narciso kissed her, hoping he had reassured her. He climbed upon Haro.

They were well into the frontier when Raúl spoke. "Guadalupe doesn't like it when you're gone. You know, she sees beyond the shadows, too."

"She's pregnant and filled with strong emotions, that's all," Narciso excused the implications. "When she delivers, I'll plan something to look forward to; a celebration for the baby's baptism." Narciso paused and looked at Raúl, "Let's hurry this mission before Los Indios notice that the men are away from home."

Narciso rode in silence while considering a strategy. He would consult with his uncle, Captain Tomás Sánchez. Since Tío Tomás founded the town of Laredo, it had grown into a thriving community.

Perhaps he could advise Narciso on the church's construction, what to name it, and how to recruit a Catholic priest.

Guadalupe delivered José Lino in 1794. That same year, the Franciscan Friars opened the doors to a new mission on the Texas coast less than 100 miles from the Agostadero. Narciso traveled to Nuestra Señora del Refugio Church, returning with a priest for the baby's baptism. The appearance of a Padre was the chance for the community to engage him for confessions, bless the newly established ranches and the animals, solemnize unions not yet consecrated in the Catholic Church, and christen the new baby and those never baptized. It was baptisms that secured families. By choosing madrinas and padrinos, godparents for their children, parents secured life-long bonds with compadres, who, in the event of their death, promised to raise their godchild as their own in the teachings of the Catholic faith. Finally, the Padre arranged an outdoor Mass, culminating in a much-needed benediction that filled the community with euphoria and hope for the future. With the help of the women in the community, Narciso made good on his pledge and hosted a grand celebration. Guadalupe, with the newborn in her arms, watched from the veranda. She smiled as the festival grew boisterous with singing and dancing, lasting well into the early morning.

Before the year ended, Narciso's community now included landowners.

He designated and pledged to relatives, vaqueros, and devoted Indians who came with their families that the land he deeded was theirs to own and develop in perpetuity.

Chapter 11

MEMORIES OF MEXICO

Auntie and I grabbed a quick breakfast after checking out of the hotel in Tampico. We still smiled over the fuss the young porter made over Auntie's GTO. She put the top down, and we saw dawn on the horizon. Auntie drove, leaving the city behind; I turned to get a final view of Tampico's beautiful French and Art Nouveau buildings. She followed Hwy 80, and I recognized the signs for the small towns we passed on our drive back to the Border; Miramar, Altimira, Villa Manuel, and the 101 highway that showed us on course to Matamoros/Brownsville. We would cross into the United States in six hours, marking the end of our six-day Mexican excursion.

"We'll first drop off our luggage at a hotel in Brownsville, then walk across to Matamoros." Auntie sounded excited but changed her tone when she caught my look of alarm at crossing the border again. "It's our last hurrah. Don't you want to visit the shops at the border and haggle with the vendors?"

I remembered strolling through the booths displaying straw purses, guayabera shirts, dresses embellished with vivid embroidered flowers, ornate, exquisitely stitched pillowcases, leather handbags, and sandals popular in Mexico—Huaraches.

"I'm not ready to say goodbye to Mexico again," I murmured.

"You remember your past visits?" Auntie asked but seemed to understand my feelings.

"Mama and Daddy traveled many times to Mexico. This trip reminded me of how unique and special Mexico can be. I remember our parents first brought John and me as children."

She turned to look at me, "Tell me about Mexico with your father, Chon.I used to go with them when your parents visited the Hacienda before you and Juanito were born."

I smiled at her reference to my brother and replied, "I didn't know you visited Sabinas."

"…what do you remember as a child," she urged, "I must admit, it's way too early, so help me stay awake by entertaining me with a story." I snickered and began to sort out my memories.

"The first time we went to Mexico was in 1955; John and I were eight and seven. We both sensed our parent's excitement, and it rubbed off. Laredo was the border town with Nuevo Laredo, the first Mexican town we entered on our way to Sabinas Hidalgo, Nuevo Leon, Mexico. "We boarded a Greyhound bus in Galveston for Laredo."

She gave a wide grin, "That sounds like fun."

"My parents packed a lot of luggage. Things like cigarettes, handkerchiefs, sheets, and towels. They also encouraged John and me to pack toys we no longer played with in a suitcase filled with new toys my parents had placed on layaway for the kids in Mexico." I looked at Auntie and made a face.

"It made you jealous that the kids got new toys, right? It does sound like a lot of suitcases," Auntie agreed.

"Yeah," I responded, "we were brats."

"In Laredo, the customs agent examined every piece of luggage. I remember a slight commotion when he opened the largest bag filled with groceries. Mama took canned goods, dry cereal, powdered and canned evaporated milk, peanut butter, jelly, canned tuna, and chlorine dioxide tablets, a disinfectant to treat water for drinking. The agent was gruff when he saw the food and asked Mama, "Where are you taking this food?" Mama pointed and nodded toward us kids. The agent smiled and closed the bag. Once cleared for travel, we were ready to board a bus to Monterrey. The attendant told Daddy that the first stop was in Sabinas."

"Why did the agent question the food, I wonder," Auntie asked.

I shrugged my shoulders. "I noticed the bus waiting for the passengers to go through inspection was nothing like the Greyhound bus. It looked like it was once a school bus, but in faded white paint, the words Autobús de México stenciled on the outside."

"The bus driver waited until the inspection was over. That must have taken a long time."

"I'm not sure," I said. "but he didn't seem anxious nor fidgety about having to wait."

"How was the bus ride getting there?" Auntie giggled, and I could tell she knew about Mexican travel.

I rolled my eyes, "Oh my gosh, the bus ride was frightening." In 1955, there were no highways to Sabinas.

Auntie giggled, "Tell me about the bus. I drove that road every time I went to Monterrey."

Mustering a sobering look, I turned to face her, "First of all, Daddy told us we'd be riding first class. We didn't know what that meant, but it sounded exciting."

Laughing, Auntie said, "That meant you sat in front of the bus, away from the people who brought their goats, chickens, and piglets on board, right?"

"Yes," I laughed too.

"And the ride to the top of the mountain?" I could tell she already knew the answer.

"You know the route well if you remember that mountain."

Auntie laughed. "Cuesta De Mamulique Carretera, which means the

Slope of Mamulique Road."

"A slope? Was that mountain called a slope? Boy, that's an understatement! That slope was where John and I thought we'd die." I looked at Auntie, who was enjoying the conversation.

"...and it was a plush ride, right?" Auntie giggled.

"No! The bus was a rust bucket on four bald tires, the doors flapped on their hinges like they were caught in a cyclone, and small holes in certain floorboard areas showed the gravel road whooshing by underneath us." Auntie started to giggle but laughed aloud as I continued.

"The driver must have taken lessons at the Indianapolis 500 Speedway because whenever he circled the mountain, the bus felt like it leaned on two wheels; it rattled and shook like it was caught in the gale of a hurricane. The animals in the bus squawked and bleated, and I buried my face into Daddy's chest after I saw the plunge at the next turn if the bus tumbled off the road."

Auntie could not contain her laughter. "Weren't Tila and Chon worried?"

"No, they behaved as if this was all normal. Daddy closed his eyes like he was dozing, and Mama read us a book."

Auntie chuckled. "I remember that drive."

"It took an hour and a half to get to Sabinas, but we arrived in great spirits. Daddy whistled to attract the attention of a row of taxi drivers waiting for a customer and hired two to take us to Tío Manual and Tía Elva's."

"Two?" Auntie questioned.

"I went with Mama and John with Daddy; we had a lot of luggage," I clarified.

Auntie nodded, then stopped to put up the top to protect us from the rising sun's rays. "Keep going," she insisted, returning to the road.

"Relatives filled Tío and Tía's house. We watched as they ran down the front steps with wide smiles and open arms to greet us. The radio station announced our visit because that's how everyone in town knew what was going on."

She chuckled, "You're serious," and I nodded.

"Yes, the local radio station that announced birthdays, births and baptisms, the latest death, a funeral, all matter of information, announced our visit, so everyone in town knew what was going on."

"The whole town knew you'd be arriving." Auntie smiled, "That's nice."

"I'm sure of it. We arrived by taxi, and everyone, even relatives from surrounding little towns, knew just when to meet at Tío and Tía's."

"Maybe the taxi driver called ahead to let them know," Auntie suggested. I tried to recall, "I don't remember a telephone in the house."

"You know, your dad's brother, Manuel, was the youngest, and I remember him in the early 1940s dating Elva—they were just teenagers back then."

"Really? They had two kids then. Ramon, the oldest, was ten, and Gloria was five. My folks, John and I, everybody got caught up in the commotion of hugs and kisses."

Auntie smiled as if remembering a romantic scene. "Yeah," she said, "I remember how the family all got together to say hello."

"Exactly," I confirmed. "Everyone treated us like," I couldn't find the right words, "as if we were special, like celebrities. They appreciated every gift, small or large, new, or used. Every day, someone planned a fun-filled day. That's how they gave back for the gifts— with dinners at other people's homes or a gathering at the Plaza to hear musicians sing and dance. Or a day at Ojo de Agua. It was exciting."

"Yep, that's what I remember about Chon's family; generous and fun-loving people. So, the whole town joined in welcoming the Esquivel family, with one celebration after another; woohoo," Auntie cheered, which made me laugh.

"We, John and I, sensed that my parents were special."

She grinned widely and asked, "How did that make you feel?"

"Like we were royalty."

"That's because you are," Auntie interjected, and I smiled. The stories already sounded boastful, and I'd never heard about conquistadors in my history classes. I didn't want to talk about famous ancestors because I still had difficulty believing my ancestry.

"We were the family from el otro lado," the other side.

"El Norte, the dream of every struggling and poor Mexican," Auntie added.

"I loved the house Tío and Tía owned in Sabinas, a sturdy four-room stucco house that remained as cool inside as it was outside. Even from the neighborhood, the kids slept outdoors underneath the large, covered porch in the cool evening breeze. Plush feather-filled wool blankets served as mattresses. In the morning, the aroma of freshly made corn tortillas roused us kids. We'd wander into the large kitchen while Tía Elva removed a masa dough ball, patted it flat in her hands, and cooked it. When it was our turn, she'd handed us each a taco filled with fresh avocado slices.

Auntie smiled and nodded. "What a treat! Where did she get the avocados?"

"The backyard was full of trees, some the size of an oak, filled with avocados."

Auntie looked at me incredulously, "An avocado tree as big as an oak?"

I nodded, "That's what I remember. I was little, and the trees looked huge."

We were quiet for a moment. The bright rays of sunlight caressed the landscape. We passed the beautiful region of Mexico, a deserted coastline. I wondered if people lived beyond the marsh on the opposite side of the ocean. I could imagine peaceful and tranquil colonies by the sea similar to those that existed for my family in Sabinas when I was seven years old.

"What else do you remember?" Auntie asked. "Take me back to those days."

"We'd eat breakfast and, afterward, wash and brush our teeth in the faucet off the front porch. At night we'd bathed using that same faucet in a large wash tub with only our underpants on. We'd pull on clean play clothes—not pajamas—to wear the next day. Tía always prepared an early supper for the kids with homemade tortillas."

"What a treat," Auntie exclaimed.

"All the kids, including neighborhood playmates, sat around the table laughing and talking like we had something important to discuss. If the food wasn't to our liking, such as when John refused to eat breakfast because Mexican chickens laid the eggs, Mama pulled out the emergency stash."

"I love that," Auntie laughed. "I remember the time when I babysat. I made oatmeal—Tila said you two ate oatmeal—and I decorated it; coconut for hair, raisins for eyes, and pecans for the mouth."

"I remember that breakfast," I smiled.

"Yes," Auntie laughed again, "Juanito picked off all the decorations, and when you saw him, you did too."

Justifying my actions, I responded, "He was the older brother."

"What did your parents do while you kids wandered the neighborhood?"

"Daddy took off with his brothers and cousins to La Hacienda. Mama brought along a wool blanket that needed refurbishing. Tía gathered the neighborhood women to recover it with new fabric. Somebody brought a frame, and the women covered the old fabric with the new one. They'd sit outside to watch us play while they hand-stitched, talked, and laughed on the porch."

"Those were the days," Auntie said under her breath.

"We explored the whole village. Back then, Sabinas was a tiny town with a central plaza, an unfinished Catholic Church, and shops.

"A simpler life," Auntie exclaimed.

"The shops in downtown Sabinas were buildings, not makeshift booths. There was a Mercado with meat hanging on racks," I looked at Auntie as she nodded, "like a clothesline, tables with pig heads for tamales, buckets of pigs' feet for Menudo, baskets with fresh produce, canned goods, and cleaning supplies against the wall.

Outside, a large wash tub on a fire pit filled with cooking oil fried chicharónes. I tasted a sample of the most delicious candy at this market, Leche Quemada. I now know the ingredients; brown and white sugar, butter, evaporated milk, vanilla, and nuts, boiled together, when the consistency of fudge, poured to cool, and cut into squares."

"You're making me hungry." Auntie interrupted, "Want to stop and get something?"

The sun had risen to its highest position in the sky, the noon hour. We saw a marker for towns on the Gulf of Mexico and chose one called Carvajal.

"We have Carvajal relatives. Let's see if we bump into one," Auntie teased, "after all, it's our last fling in an old Mexican village."

We drove into a tiny fishing town with half a dozen structures facing the water. Toward the center of the row of huts sat an open-air stall. Smoke from the grill emitted the best-smelling aroma. We approached an elderly couple; the woman was dressed in a faded blue loose-fitting top and skirt, the man in faded blue jeans and a bright blue guayabera. Their faces were weathered from too much sunshine, salt air, and sand. We assumed they were locals and greeted them.

"Soy Sra. Eloisa Diaz, y Barbara es me sobrina," she introduced us, and they, in turn, said they were Feliciano and Jacinta. Feliciano's eyes looked past us to Auntie's car and whispered something to Jacinta. Jacinta's bright eyes seemed to dance at her husband's comment.

Auntie smiled, "You're the owners?" she asked in Spanish, pointing to the grill and asking if we could purchase something to eat.

"No, not a business," Feliciano answered. "My wife and I cook for the people who come in from fishing. They provide the catch, and we cook a meal."

"It smells delicious," Auntie said, and we looked at the grill filled with bell pepper, squash, onion, sliced tomatoes, shrimp, and fish."

Jacinta stood from the table and reached for a bowl filled with corn masa balls. She patted a ball between her weathered hands, expertly turning it into a perfect circle, then dropped it on a griddle to cook. She repeated the process until at least six tortillas were cooked.

Feliciano then stepped to the grill, tossed the food, and set up a flare of sizzle, steam, and aromas. "Want a taco?"

Auntie looked at me. With eyes opened wide, I nodded. The food smelled delicious, my growling belly signaling I was ravenous.

"Both my niece and I will have a taco if you don't mind," Auntie told them.

"Es un placer," Feliciano answered, turning toward Jacinta, who smiled and nodded. "Our pleasure. We don't usually get visitors in Carvajal."

Auntie told him we were looking for a place to eat and saw the town named after our ancestor, Luis de Carvajal, who, in 1579, King Phillip of Spain awarded a large territory in Mexico. He looked at Auntie, smiled, and nodded. I held my breath. "Lo entiendo." He understood. This modest and kind man never responded rudely to our arrogance. He didn't need to be schooled in the history of our ancestors, but I didn't mention it to Auntie.

Jacinta placed a paper plate with a generously filled taco in front of me. She gestured with her hand if I wanted something to drink. When I responded in Spanish, Jacinta smiled. She took out a bottled Coke and opened it. Auntie sat next to me and said she'd have one with her taco. The flavor was delicious, and I savored every bite. When we finished, Feliciano asked if we'd like another, and we both said no. Auntie opened her purse and insisted on giving them something for the food, but he kept waving his hand and nodding no.

"We don't pay for the fish, and we get more than we eat," he told her.

Consider this meal a gift in homage to your ancestor."

Auntie nodded, clearly embarrassed at this humble fisherman's hospitality.

"May we use the facilities before we get on the road?" she asked.

The couple snickered, then stopped, and placed a hand over their mouths. They looked at each other, then back to us.

"You'll probably do better finding a nice, clear brush-free spot on the road," Feliciano answered.

"I have toilet paper," Auntie told him.

The couple once again looked at each other, and Feliciano mumbled under his breath. He looked at us and replied, "Get your paper."

Jacinta took us to a crude outhouse far from nearby structures whose wooden frames had seen better days. I prepared for the worst conditions, and my expectations were spot-on. Instead of a door, a plastic shower curtain hung precariously on two hooks. The wooden toilet seat looked rough, scratchy, and uninviting, but at least I didn't have to squat—I hovered over the opening. When we left, I noticed Auntie placed the toilet paper on a nearby rock with money neatly folded inside the cylinder.

Satisfied, gratified, and relieved, we left the cool, refreshing breeze of the beach and headed back to the 101 highway.

"Jacinta and Feliciano are like the people I know in Mexico," I told Auntie.

"Neighborly?" Auntie questioned, and I nodded.

"They're kind, generous, and accepting of our quirks; they treated us with such kindness." Auntie nodded.

"On that first trip to Mexico when I was seven, we had a special playmate—a boy called Feliz. I thought it was because he was always smiling, but later I learned his name was Feliciano. I noticed because, like me, he was different."

Auntie turned her gaze and looked at me.

"He was different in another way, but, like me, he stood out from the other children. The group accepted him, although he may have been a couple of years older than my ten-year-old cousin. He happily played with the children no matter the age and went inside a playmate's house as if he belonged there. I saw him sitting at the large table of a restaurant dinner party in our honor. He appeared as part of the group everywhere I looked. I couldn't understand. I always had to ask permission to play outside with my friends.

Mama never allowed us to enter a neighbor's house, even if we asked permission. I wondered what made this boy so special.

"Who does he belong to?" I asked Tía Elva. "She answered, 'He belongs to all of us.' At first, her answer confused me. How did he belong to all of us? I'd watch him. He was there at meals with the kids because it didn't matter whom you belonged to; we ate together.

He smiled and was friendly, and his clothes were always neat and clean. He had reddish-orange hair, a freckled face, and blue eyes. He didn't look like any of us—we all had dark hair, brown or hazel eyes, and various skin tones from light to dark. I later learned this boy was born with Down's Syndrome."

Auntie breathed loudly, "Wow, did you ever learn who his parents were?"

"No, " Tía's response that he belonged to everyone intrigued me for years. In time, I understood her to mean we are all responsible for our actions toward one another and never to bully or ignore people, including those with infirmities. I noticed that none of the kids made him the center of attention because he was different.

Children or adults never pointed fingers or stared at his features. He ate at the house he was in when it was time to eat. Someone gave him clean clothes if he was dirty, and he took his turn to bathe in the wash tub like the rest of us. At night, if he decided to, he slept with the gang of kids on the front porch. Similarly, the kids never treated me like I was different. One time a girl asked me why I wore such heavy shoes and what were those attachments sticking out of them. I answered her, and that was the end of it. Like this boy, no one ever treated me like an outcast."

"You never forgot," Auntie commented.

"No," I whispered, "such a contrast to back home. Our neighborhood had lots of kids. We'd gather in the street, ride bikes, and play together. A girl named Janet rode her bike to be around us. She had cyst-like bumps all over her body and was slightly mentally challenged, but when she tried to be part of the group, the kids ridiculed her instead of welcoming her. She and I bonded one summer when casts on both legs confined me to the front porch."

"What did you and Janet do?" Auntie's voice turned soft.

Thinking about Janet brought a wave of recall of that hot, muggy day in July when I craved comfort and Janet needed an ally.

"She'd sit atop her bike, lean against our fence, and we'd talk. She never asked to join me on the porch; she never came inside our house. Around three o'clock, she'd go home and didn't return until the next day."

"What did you talk about?" Auntie asked softly.

"I usually sat outside with a book. Janet would ask about the story, and I'd give her a report on whatever I was reading." Auntie and I smiled, and I continued.

"I don't remember what we talked about." It made me sad to think about Janet as I recalled her awkward gait, isolation, and soft and gentle nature. My eyes began to tear. "I only remember how cruel the other kids were. Once I asked Mama why the kids were so mean, and Mama said, 'Because she is special.' Mama later explained that people often made excuses for people with disabilities by blaming the condition on God's imposed punishment for a past wrong. She told me she didn't believe handicaps resulted from a vengeful God. However, it didn't stop people challenged by their lives from finding a secret relief in someone worse off than them. I told Mama I still didn't understand, and she told me to look at Janet's personality, 'she has an angel's heart and beautiful innocent eyes.' Mama was right about her; Janet never talked about anyone or complained about being mistreated."

Auntie changed her tone, "What made you want to know such things, Querida?"

I smiled, "I don't know. I never understood cruelty—not toward animals, children, and especially for bodily defects or flaws a person had no control over. Bullying made me standoffish and reserved to the point that older cousins accused me of being a snob. But I also remember grown-ups looking at me—as if I was contagious, while their children pointed and snickered. Instead of teaching the child, the parent stared at me, turning in another direction as if brushing against me might contaminate her children."

Auntie whispered, "That's horrible."

★

We arrived at the border late afternoon, and the agent checked our luggage. It was a relief when he allowed me to cross into Texas with only my driver's license. He was in awe of Auntie's car, and this time she didn't press our luck. She answered all his questions, opened the hood, and even showed him the button to put the top down. In Brownsville, we stayed in the same hotel as before.

Auntie and I had a similar room with two twin beds. We laid down, and before long, both of us slept. When I woke, Auntie was looking through the phone book.

"I found La Fonda, just across the border into Matamoros. She looked for my reaction.

We're going to walk across to Mexico for a meal; we won't need to go through any paper shuffling." I didn't say anything because I wasn't comfortable navigating the border a third time since I didn't have a birth certificate indicating I was a U.S. citizen.

"This is the last time we'll see Mexico, Auntie cajoled. Besides, one margarita will soothe all anxiety.

We entered the familiar office at the border crossing and were the only people wanting to pass through. I thought of Manuel from our initial entry and hoped he wasn't on duty. I stayed close to the door, far enough away from Auntie that I couldn't hear the conversation. Auntie approached the counter to chat with the agent authorizing passes. I felt my heart begin to beat faster and my nervous level rise. Once again, Auntie was convincing a government agent to let me cross the border without any papers.

As I watched the goings on, Auntie tilted back her head and roared with laughter. Then she leaned onto the counter and grinned as if conveying secrets. The agent, in turn, nodded and laughed uproariously. He'd slap the counter as if she told a good joke. I watched this back and forth between Auntie and the agent. That seemed to take an hour, but ten minutes later, Auntie had in hand the necessary paper.

"Adios," she waved him a backward goodbye.

In a matter of minutes, we were at the restaurant, settled with those delicious margaritas while waiting for our orders. I slurped mine slowly to avoid getting a headache. Auntie had a knack for getting her way, and I marveled at how people responded.

I bit the top of my straw to slow the intake as I sucked the margarita. "How'd you do it?"

"Wha, how'd I do what?" Auntie gave me a puzzled look.

"How did you convince the agent to let me cross?" She was downplaying the encounter with the agent because I'd been so nervous.

"Oh, you know, I used my feminine charm," she answered, holding back a smile.

"Auntie," I slurped and exhaled, "How did you do it? If I've learned anything about you, it's your ingenuity. I want to learn from you."

"Oh. Well, um, I just told him I was dropping my criada back home to her parents," she said in a teasing tone.

As I choked on my margarita, Auntie had to slap my back. She'd told the agent she was returning her house cleaner to her parent's home.

"He believed you were a little servant girl by watching you cowering at the door."

We were both giddy as we walked across the bridge to the U.S. side and to Auntie's parked car. "Another perfect day," I expressed to Auntie.

"I'm looking forward to that pillow," Auntie replied. She had indulged in two Margaritas.

That night, I was asleep before my head hit the pillow. It was the best night's slumber, and Auntie and I woke up in great moods.

The following day, Auntie remarked, "We didn't get to go shopping." I didn't say anything because I felt we had pushed our luck. Next time, I'd be jailed for not having proper documents to prove I was an American citizen.

Auntie handed me my driver's license. "It's daylight, those border agents can tell you're American. Let's go shopping."

Later that afternoon, we walked across the bridge to our hotel, passing into the U.S. side without interference.

"By the way," Auntie said, "we haven't talked much about her, but Guadalupe is one of those women who instilled a lot of independence and strength in the Cavazos women. You should know more about her."

Chapter 12

GUADALUPE

After reading the map, we followed Hwy 77 from Brownsville to San Antonio through the town once called the pasture of San Juan de Carricitos. Auntie began talking about Cavazos's documents that still existed.

"If you look into Narciso's papers, there are accounts that José Lino was a foster child to Narciso and Guadalupe. I don't know what happened to his mother, but he's important in your history, Querida because he's the one who inherited La Hacienda de Los Cavazos."

"Daddy's side of the family inherited the hacienda because of José Lino?"

Auntie looked at me with her lips pursed and nodded yes.

"I thought Teresa and José Blas were twins since both were born the same year, but José Lino was born when Teresa and Blas were two. Who keeps track of those records?"

"The Catholic Church," Auntie responded. "The official baptismal record lists José Lino as a foster child on your father's Cavazos line and your grandmother's Esquivel family. José Lino's the one who inherited La Hacienda de Los Cavazos in Mexico, where your father was born and raised. He may have been Narciso's grandson, nephew, or godson.

I wasn't sure I understood. "How do you keep all this information straight?"

"Church records and family talk. Your Esquivel grandmother nursed at least two or three babies after their mothers died in childbirth or had milk fever. The women who died were close family; the child brought into the household and raised as their own was a nephew, a niece, or a godchild. Women nursed their babies for a couple of years, some for three years, so a woman might still produce milk when a sister or cousin died in childbirth."

"But how do we know that's what happened with José Blas?"

Auntie laughed, "He was family—and that's all that counts. Okay, see if this helps. Over the decades, the Hacienda passed to your grandmother, an Esquivel, who married your grandfather, an Inclán."

"Why didn't the family take the Inclán name? Why am I, Esquivel?"

"In the olden days, children decided which surname they'd take. You'll find that the girls often took their mothers, while the boys took their fathers. The majority chose the more influential pedigree," Auntie laughed.

I was confused. "An influential surname? What does that mean?"

Auntie was enjoying telling the tale. Her face was soft, and her eyes looked dreamy as if she were in a different time.

"Way back when it had to do with connections to the elite families of Spain. That's why King Charles IV awarded Narciso a massive grant; because of family connections."

All I knew of the Inclán name was that Daddy was a descendant of the First Families of Bexar County. "So, the stories Mama told us that we descend from King Ferdinand IV are true."

"That's right. These early ancestors knew their family history and which name had clout." I shook my head. So much to take in.

"Remember, Querida," Auntie looked at me and grinned, "there was no television. Storytelling was entertainment—as well as other activities," she wiggled her eyebrows. I turned and faced the road. I knew what she meant.

"Also," Auntie continued, "we are direct descendants of Guadalupe. She could be our grandmother or aunt. Narciso is a cousin."

I didn't say anything. I liked the idea of having Guadalupe as a close relative and began rethinking my academic goals. My major was biology, with plans for a medical career in Physical Therapy. That involved transferring to Baylor College in Waco, Texas, after my junior year. I needed to delve into History—Spain and the role of Spain in the Americas. Genealogy was like learning another foreign language.

"I should change my major to History," I remarked.

Auntie looked at me and scrunched her face, "History? Nah, there's no money in research, and there will always be sick people." She squeezed my arm and said, "Remember, I'm going to tell you about Guadalupe. You're gonna like her story."

We had to take a country road to get to the small towns of Sebastian, Lyford, and Raymondville. I settled comfortably into my seat. With the top down, I imagined I was on a magic carpet ride, looking upon what was once the Agostadero.

★

It took Guadalupe almost six months, but by the end of 1794, she learned to adapt to the sights, sounds, and smells of the wilderness. When she heard the prairie wolves howling their mournful bays to distant packs, these coyotes sounded as if they were outside the door. She'd lay awake for hours, heart thumping, for the beasts to tear down the door viciously. She eventually learned to calm herself to the deep breathing sounds of her family, snuggled and safe in their beds. She'd move closer to Narciso and placed their newest, José Lino, between them. José Blas and Teresa were two years old; the boy shared a bed with four-year-old Jorge, and Clara with three-year-old Teresa. Ignacia had a curtained area at the corner of the house.

Guadalupe listened to the comforting reassurances of her husband's breathing. Life here was so different from home in Mexico; she thought, I have status. She was la Doña, the woman everyone came to with their problems and for advice. She smiled, no longer considered a girl but a woman. When she told Ela, the vaquero Vicente's wife, that she finally felt like a grown-up when she turned twenty-one, Ela teased her and said she was a girl until her fiftieth birthday. Guadalupe turned her face into the pillow to muffle her laugh. Narciso breathed in and turned, and she moved slightly, giving him and José Lino more space.

She thought about their romance and how quickly they had become involved. She was just a girl then and knew nothing about men. Twenty-three years older than she, Narciso repeatedly told her he felt awkward and clumsy. "You're beautiful, and you're young; find someone more your age to love." She sighed deeply, remembering those bumbling moments. "I know how I feel", she would respond.

Turning on her back, she looked at the darkened ceiling. Before Narciso, she had never experienced love; those intense feelings, deep affection, and the passionate force driving away all rational thought. Narciso and his family were in turmoil when she encountered the family in mourning after Maria Ignacia's sudden death. No one seemed to notice little eleven-year-old Ignacia struggling as if lost in the wild, far from help. She took the little girl under her wing, comforted her, and wrapped her in an embrace when grief became overwhelming. She noticed that Narciso, too, wore a confused look. He'd gazed at his four children in that same distress, knowing they were suffering but confused about which one to comfort first.

I don't know how to help them; he told Guadalupe. I don't know how to help myself.

She noticed that he began to watch her whenever she calmed Ignacia. Then, more and more, Narciso began disrupting his routine so he could spend time around Guadalupe, catching up with her when she was alone. Before long, her feelings for Narciso surfaced—she was in love. Her parents already had a marriage partner in mind for when she turned eighteen in another year. Could she defy them with her choice, her happiness? She would decide, knowing she would have to live with the unpleasant results. Fate brought Narciso and her together, and her heart demanded love instead of loyalty to society's rules.

She was the early riser and kept a basket with her toilette near the door.

She thought about her parents and how fortunate she was that their thinking was more enlightened. She reflected on her girlhood—the time she overheard her parents discussing whether or not to hire a tutor to teach fourteen-year-old Guadalupe the basics. She had leaned close to the room where their voices rose and fell as each parent held their ground.

"She's a girl," Mamá told Papá; she doesn't need to learn to read or write.

Tutoring is not for girls. It'll only make the local women think Guadalupe is better than their daughters. How about our daughter, Ana, whom we never considered educating? Won't she get jealous?" Ana was Guadalupe's only sibling, ten years older, married, and living with her family.

Papá responded, softly trying to convince his wife. "Ana will completely understand. Look at you, Maria, wouldn't it be easier to manage this Hacienda when I'm traveling for a month? Arithmetic, reading, and writing are essential for everyone. How else will you know what you're being charged for and if the prices are fair?"

"Those decisions wait for when you are home. Now stop this silly talk," Mamá told Papá, "I'm too old to interrupt my busy schedule with reading."

She heard Papá sigh. "That's why I say, let's educate Guadalupe while she's still young. We don't know where life will take her; it's better to prepare than keep her ignorant. We could both die tomorrow, and she's left to run the Hacienda with a fortune hunter looking to take advantage."

Mamá was quiet for a long time. Guadalupe thought that Mamá was stewing over Papá's, hinting that she, Mamá, was ignorant because she couldn't read or write. The girls in Guadalupe's circle of friends were illiterate. In Mexico, girls only learned to recite prayers and say the rosary. Reading was off-limits because the Church believed that if girls learned to read and write, they'd pollute their minds by reading condemned books. They might also receive or write love letters from an inappropriate suitor, forbidden by parents who chose the marriage partner.

The Doña would instruct servants on the formal table setting, a function Mamá had taught Guadalupe at an early age for dining with officials. But girls only needed to learn refined skills like embroidery, crochet, and painting. Running a house was considered a necessary but indelicate duty. However, that's why the Doña hired servants, who butchered small animals, did all the cooking, and served the meals.

Papá succeeded. He convinced Mamá to educate Guadalupe. From age twelve to fifteen, she spent three times a week with her tutor, a novitiate from San Luis Rey de Francia in Monterrey, Mexico.

What a pious, solemn young man, she thought. It's a good thing, or I wouldn't have learned anything.

Guadalupe thought about the first poem she read of her ancestor, Rodrigo Díaz de Vivar, *Cantar de mío Cid*, and wondered, will stories be written of the conquistadors of Mexico? After all, it's been almost two centuries since Spain conquered the Aztecs.

She walked barefoot on the cool, dewy grass and washed in the stream by their cabin from the Laguna Madre. The water, like the air, was cool and crisp. She looked deep into the thick brush and grassland on the other side of the stream and watched for any movement. All this open land hid onlookers, whether they be beasts or men.

Satisfied she was alone, she slipped off her nightdress and stepped into the stream that fed off the Rio Grande, peering into the clear, clean water to see speckled trout startled by her presence. This was fair play, she smiled. Sometimes, while reaching for the gradually growing light after night's darkness, a jumping trout would startle her cheered on by the start of day.

Today, no small creatures greeted her, although there were times when she would surprise elk or porcupines. Once, she especially enjoyed watching a family of armadillos scamper into the grassland. Such strange little creatures, she told Narciso; they are like the conquistadors of the past and wear battle armor. Narciso enjoyed the analogy and laughed out loud.

Occasionally, when she rose from her bath, she felt eyes watching her. She stared deep into the thicket, hoping to catch a glimpse—the whites of an eye or the glint of a shiny object. She hesitated to worry Narciso about this. The Indians, she reasoned, were more interested in the available livestock to feed their families. In her eyes, the few they took didn't affect the number of calves born regularly on the rich grazing land of the Agostadero. If an Indian did watch her, he knew how to become part of the overgrowth— blend into the landscape, dead still, no matter how hard she looked.

Guadalupe was grateful when Narciso and Raúl gathered the women and taught them to shoot their long guns with a flintlock and how to manage a knife in case Indians attacked the women when the men were too far away.

Guadalupe came to rely on Raúl and his Native ways, which made sense in this wilderness. His ancestors were the Tlaxcaltecs, who assisted Hernán Cortés in defeating the Aztecs. With sparkling blue eyes, pale skin, and jet-black hair, the generations of marriages between the Spaniards and the native population erased Raúl's Native features. However, he remained close to his traditions possessing a spiritual lifestyle, healing practices, and deep respect for nature.

Raúl introduced Narciso to the medicine woman, Ela, who helped Raúl to comfort and relieve foaling horses and first calf heifers.

Guadalupe touched her now flat belly. When she went into labor with José Lino, the first baby born in the Agostadero, Ela helped with the childbirth.

Guadalupe breathed in deeply, inhaling the smells of the wilderness, the fresh air free of animal odor, and dusty desert paths. She savored the sumptuous earthy scent of new timber and wild vegetation.

After washing, Guadalupe rubbed her body with flower oils and waters distilled from the blooms of roses, orange flowers, and jasmine. She treasured this simple life, opposite to what she had left behind. The women who accompanied them taught her their secret blending techniques for making fragrances, and, in return, she led the women to read and write.

She put on a clean muslin frock and turned full circle to take in her surroundings. She never felt fearful and instead embraced native survival skills from those who accompanied them. At the Agostadero, nature abounded, giving them and the families in the community everything they needed; relationships became true friendships. Her life at her parent's Hacienda never had this kind of female intimacy. Guadalupe thought back to her girlhood companions. What a silly and frivolous group. She thought about how they had ridiculed her when she told them she would help with her cousin's household when his wife died. "The family is in shock;" she told her friends, "my cousin, Narciso, doesn't know how to cope, and the children, my cousins, they're grieving for their Mamá."

"They have servants," her friends responded, unmoved by the death of a young wife and mother. "You don't need to dirty your hands." But the grief Guadalupe saw and felt, the confusion Narciso and her young cousins showed, convinced her that she had to help. She took little Ignacia under her wing and let the little girl grieve for a mother who died too soon. With Guadalupe there, Ignacia coped. Ignacia, she thought with a smile, was such a treasure. "She never wanted me to leave La Hacienda when it was time to go back home."

Later, when she and Narciso became involved, Narciso's three adult children had mixed emotions; they got married and left home. "To escape the gossip," she wondered. She bore four children before she and Narciso legally married while still living in her father's home. The Catholic Church took its time giving a dispensation. She didn't understand why permission was necessary. "For centuries families intermarried within family lines, and only now did Narciso and I need a dispensation." [9]

The neighbors scandalized over her affair, had no longer allowed their daughters to socialize with Guadalupe. Her parents, distressed at the scandal, kept her isolated. They didn't want her to hear the gossip or risk her being treated shamefully in public. Typical comments persisted; Her parents must place her in a nunnery. Or an Abbess would require her to kneel in hours-long prayers to castigate her carnal urges. The worst one was that those bastard children should be placed in homes far away from godly society. They were an established family who deserved to hold their family close, no matter the circumstances. This intolerable practice by conquistadors who sent their mestizos babies from their mother's culture to grow up in Spanish homes far removed from their Mexican Indian roots was unacceptable to Guadalupe's parents.

Guadalupe brought her thoughts back to the present. Disgrace and gossip were far behind her now. When families followed Narciso, they brought companions and partners to this land. Because of these women, she became accomplished at performing previously unknown tasks for her family, like cooking and planting a garden.

Guadalupe looked into the stream mirroring her image, pulled her waist- length hair together, divided it into three long strands, and then weaved the long tresses into a single braid. She then wrapped the bundled hair at the nape of her neck and secured it with a sheer ribbon. Smiling at her reflection, she picked up her basket to begin her morning routine.

She opened the gate to the kitchen garden to gather vegetables and herbs for breakfast. In a concert, the sound of bees buzzing around her orchid of daisies, peonies, roses, and sunflowers greeted her.

Sauntering amongst the rows of lush growing plants, a mixture of rich colors, she thought how like these plants, her life had blossomed precisely how she had wanted.

She and Narciso had weathered the storm, free to pursue a future without gossipmongers and busybodies. She chose her husband instead of having him picked by her father, the custom of her times. She and Narciso went beyond the contemporary norms, which, with other parents, would have banished her to a nunnery. But her parents stood by her and weathered the rumors. They held firm to the belief that la Sangre se Busca—bloodline and pedigree the primary reason for couples uniting.

Happily swinging her basket filled with greens, she made her way to the barn. Haro's stall was opened, as usual. He's off in search of a mare. She didn't worry about that cantankerous horse. The cows mooed at her presence, and she returned the greeting. "Buenos Dias, Blanca y Estrella". She kissed them before milking. Poor animals; their calves had been taken from them for their new role of supplying milk to the family. She shook her head to shed the thoughts of those baby calves slaughtered for their meat. When finished milking, she led Blanca and Estrella into the field, where they were free to roam and feast on the rich grassland.

With a bucket of milk and her basket of vegetables, she gathered eggs from the chicken coop. The chickens' chattering and shrieking grew louder as Guadalupe neared their habitat. "They behave as if they recognize I'm after their newly laid eggs," she laughed at the fuss cradling the eggs amidst the greens in the basket and thanked them, "Gracias, Gallinas' nobles," sprinkling corn as redemption.

Her last stop was an enclosure encircled by a thicket of herb foliage. She stepped inside what was, for now, a root cellar, closed the gate, and inspected the area to see if animals had breached the cage. She had learned from the Indian women that peat near the stream was perfect for cooling and preserving perishable foods. [10]

She removed salted pork for breakfast and inserted the bucket of milk to cool in the peat. She fell entirely into her day, facing upward, and pulling back her shoulders. She hummed a classic Spanish tune, *Aquella Sierra Nevada*, that other Sierra Nevada, as she made her way to the outdoor kitchen, where she placed her breakfast items on the long table facing the sunrise. Embers from the firepit still glimmered, and she blew on them to get them started, throwing in handfuls of kindling from twigs gathered in a large basket, the remains of harvested trees. She added coffee and sugar to yesterday's coffee grounds and poured water from the well water she'd drawn just before dark. Her milk came in, signaling that José Lino would soon awaken. Quickly, she began stirring water into maize hominy meal to set the dough for corn tortillas. She looked at her hands. Although still a pianist's long and slim fingers, her hands wore callouses, and lacquer no longer polished her short-cut nails. She touched her nose; it was still peeling from a sunburn.

Although she shielded her face from the sun's brutal rays, long hours outside filtered through her straw hat and tinged her face. She liked the fact that her fair skin was now more of a soft olive tone.

José Lino began sniffling, indicating he would soon announce he was awake. She approached him quickly and silently before his loud wails disturbed her sleeping family. Guadalupe held him up and kissed him. She loved how her new babies declared their presence. Each had a unique style of letting her know what they wanted, and he wanted to be fed now. She cuddled José Lino, who frantically searched for an exposed breast. "Not yet, mi Corazon, first a diaper change. She stepped onto the porch, sat in a rocking chair, and began to nurse. She smiled broadly and looked up just in time to watch golden rays as the sun entered the sky, discharging dazzling coloring to the clouds and grasslands.

Chapter 13

THE MENGER AND EL MERCADO

I couldn't help but think about Guadalupe's life and what she risked being with her lover, like my grandmother, Lucia, had done with Auntie's birth father. Both had gone to unknown destinations to start a new life with the love of their lives—definitely romantic—at least, that's what I thought when I first heard the story.

"The strength it took for Guadalupe to leave behind everything she ever knew for a dream of something better." I expressed to Auntie. "Grandmother Lucia did the same, didn't she?"

Auntie hesitated before responding. "I never thought of it that way," she admitted. "I was angry with her all the time. When we talked, I always threw it in her face how miserable José Canales was for all of us."

I didn't say anything. My aunts and uncles had appeared to have had solid marriages and were deeply religious; my cousins, though older by ten or twenty years, loved and spoiled John and me with attention. Grandmother Lucia died when my mother was nineteen. Still, I imagined her to be the formidable force behind her children.

"We don't need to stop, right?" Auntie asked, looking around. I followed her gaze and agreed. Within seconds, we went through Sebastian, the first town along the Texas Agostadero, Narciso's isolated pastureland. The marker at the entrance indicated Sebastian's population at four hundred, more a village than a town.

"Let's continue to Lyford," I said.

At Lyford, a few minutes up the road. Auntie paused at the marker, but we continued to the next town or village. All the while, I thought this was Narciso's journey, yet neither Auntie nor I wanted to stop at this tiny town.

"Onward and upward," Auntie said. "Maybe Raymondville will be the place to visit."

I thought if Sebastian and Lyford in 1967 had such small populations, how difficult must it have been for Narciso to populate the Agostadero in 1794? Raymondville was one more six-minute drive with a more significant population of nine thousand.

"What made Raymondville more successful?" I questioned.

"Has to be the industry," Auntie replied. "Sebastian and Lyford appear to be made up of small farms, while Raymondville has manufacturing that keeps it growing."

"Like what?" I asked, marveling at how different these towns were while so close together. I remembered they weren't even towns in Narciso's time.

We drove up and down the streets to get a feel for the area. I spotted a lot of churches—only one appeared to be Catholic.

"I understand communities need churches," I said, "but didn't the Catholic Church develop settlements for protection?" I mourned the loss of the Agostadero and wondered if Narciso would have succeeded had he had help from the Catholic Church.

"At first," Auntie said, "the padres counted on the King for financial support. They couldn't be independent without severing this relationship. Let me put it another way: the mission had to be a working farm—what better way to expand than with Indian labor? Converting the Indians was probably the easy part. The Indians who stayed were the ones who built the missions."

"But didn't the conquistadors build the towns, too? They wanted villages

165

to resemble the ones they came from in Spain; who paid for that?

"The conquistadors were opportunists," Auntie stated. They didn't care about converting souls, which was the padres' job. Like the Oñates, the leaders of expeditions were already rich men; that's how they financed their ships and crew. They were interested in land, minerals, and cheap labor."

"I know," I interrupted, "Native labor worked the mines."

"Yes," Auntie agreed, "but the conquistador kept the bulk of the minerals by insisting they used their money for equipment and labor. The Natives provided the labor, but the conquistadors deducted labor costs from the King's portion. Do you know how Narciso got the largest grant ever given to a Spaniard?"

I was stunned, "You mean he was as ruthless as the conquistadors?"

"No, I don't mean it like that; I was changing the subject. In Narciso's time, the land was valuable. He wasn't near precious ore—the Spaniards had long removed it. The land he wanted was then considered uninhabitable. Later, though, one hundred years later, oil was the new treasure—liquid gold as it came to be known."

"It must have taken a lot of courage to move," I said, unable to imagine leaving an established and comfortable homeland to begin a new one with nothing in the wilderness.

"San Juan de Carricitos had salt mines, important to Mexico and the U.S. during the war. But it was Narciso's ancestors--powerful and influential men who occupied key positions in areas of Mexico, Texas, New Mexico, Louisiana, and other places—who kept the Cavazos' name close to the King of Spain."

"If that's the case," I said glumly, my tone sharp, "if we were so prominent in paving the way in the Americas, why are we, Mexicans, shamed for speaking Spanish and our customs and not allowed in restaurants and other public places in some areas of Texas? Why do the Anglo people treat us like second-class citizens?"

"Have you experienced some of this?" Auntie averted her eyes from her driving to look into mine.

I hesitated before answering. In 1967, some areas of Texas had signs posted on stores and restaurants that read No Dogs, Negroes, Mexicans.

"Well, I'll give you a, for instance. My graduating class had a Negro as our valedictorian and a Mexican as a salutatorian. Our Principal made an announcement at assembly: 'For the first time in the history of this school, we have a second salutatorian.' She happened to be Anglo. Why couldn't this 'first time' allow these two girls to shine at a significant moment in the history of this high school?"

Auntie sighed deeply. "Life is hard enough, and humans tend to make it harder with decisions that only work for a privileged few. They've ignored that their ancestors were the immigrants."

We entered San Antonio's city limits, and Auntie said excitedly, "We're staying at the Menger, my favorite hotel near the Riverwalk."

Auntie's enthusiasm quickly became mine. I felt that stirring of excitement.

★

The Menger was another world, another time. I was enchanted. Directly across the Menger was another famous landmark, the Alamo. A porter took our luggage to the room. Auntie and I walked around the building constructed in 1859. Along the walls were pictures of the famous and the infamous who'd stayed at the Menger: President Teddy Roosevelt, a group of Rough Rider soldiers, and President Eisenhower. I stopped at the picture of Captain Richard King.

"It says here, Auntie, that Captain King died in one of the rooms. Wasn't the King Ranch once Narciso's land?"

Auntie left the other side of the room and came over.

"I never bothered to look at these pictures. That cabrón died at this hotel," Auntie took a slow breath. "Let's hope it's not in the room where we're staying."

I looked around to ensure no one heard Auntie's expletive against Captain King.

If Narciso's story comes first, before Captain King," I asked, "why is it that I've never heard about him until now?"

"Oooh," Auntie moaned, "Someday, someone might write about Narciso, but remember, Querida, they were real people with hopes and dreams like everybody. Whoever tells their story won't get it right; how could they? You need records, and there are no journals or diaries, but all their descendants should remember Narciso and Guadalupe as true Texas pioneers and trailblazers."

I stared at the picture of Captain King. "I'll bet there's a book someone wrote about him," I said.

"There is the original letter that still exists from the King of Spain granting the land. There are also court papers from lawsuits people brought upon Narciso's heirs."

"Lawsuits? What were those lawsuits about?" I was appalled. We walked around the room, gazing at the other pictures.

"Hmm, you might call it the downfall, which started with Spain, who tried to settle the Rio Grande for centuries."

Surprised, I turned and looked at Auntie, "Spain?"

"Well," she scrunched her face, "not exactly, but they contributed," she answered. "Early on, Spain attempted to settle the Rio Grande and failed. Those sent to build settlements would get sick with diseases and, in some cases, killed by the Indians who fought bitterly to maintain their land."

I nodded, "they were the first people." I had no idea of the history, customs, and culture of the original tribes except that they were native to this land.

"Spanish aristocrats were the people Spain first sent to the Rio Grande, kinda like Narciso, who had no idea how difficult it was to survive. For centuries, these aristocrats indulged in the creature comforts of the rich.

Narciso had to learn how to start from scratch; Texas was considered a brutal and unforgiving land."

"But Narciso brought with him so much knowledge he'd learn from La Hacienda, like cattle raising, farming, and digging aqueducts. Wasn't he at an advantage with those skills?"

"There were successes. I told you earlier about the grantees around Narciso, who got there before him. Those people prospered while constantly exposed to dangers. They learned to turn the wilderness into thriving haciendas."

"So Narciso's neighbors were part of his community, right?" I was determined to hear a happy ending, "What did they do right that Narciso didn't?"

Auntie smiled and took a deep breath. "Remember, ten years before, Narciso lost claim to another piece of land and didn't get El Agostadero until 1793, when he was forty-three years old. He started from scratch at what was considered, for the time, an advanced age. Those before him who were younger couldn't endure scraping a living from the ground up. Think about why," she stopped talking for a moment, "there was nothing in the Rio Grande that was hospitable. Grantees had to shape their region without government support and soldiers."

We stopped to look at the pictures of notables who stayed at the Menger; Babe Ruth, Mae West, Robert E. Lee, Ulysses S. Grant, and Sarah Bernhardt.

I had never given any thought to what my ancestors endured. I didn't even remember the first names of my Cavazos' great-grandparents.

Auntie continued, "People from all over came for the "free" land Mexico promised. The poorer ones, the mixed Spanish, and Indian mestizos, wanted to escape the slave-like conditions of the haciendas. But with more people occupying the Native lands, deadly fights began." She looked me in the face, "Those lasted for decades."

I was shocked at my ignorance. I wasn't even curious about this period of my history. My parents talked about it and told stories, but I took them to be just that—fanciful stories.

My mind was spinning.

Auntie watched my face and continued. "The more Mexicans that occupied the Texas Rio Grande, the more difficult it would be for the United States and France to claim Texas. Spanish Mexico wanted the land extending from Texas to include Louisiana."

"Spain sold Louisiana to France, but then France sold it to us," I was happy that I knew about this one event in U.S. history known as the Louisiana Purchase.

"Yes, the United States purchased Louisiana shortly after Narciso began building his community. Remember, Narciso occupied his land in 1793. He got the land grant in 1792. Under Spanish law, he had until 1797 to establish a community that included a hacienda, a town square, shops, and a church.

"And he had over half a million acres to do this," I said wistfully. "Do we know how many people came with him?" I asked.

"Nope. I can only guess." We know Oñate brought one hundred seventy families and two hundred soldiers to New Mexico." She hesitated, leaned in, and squinted her eyes at a picture of the newly built Menger hotel with horses and carriages parked out front. "Narciso did establish plots of land for family, however. Cavazos still live today in those areas of the Rio Grande."

"But Mama and Daddy never took us to Narciso's land," I said, "I would never have heard this story had you not made this trip—and invited me," I added quickly.

"Mexico has always been a country at war," Auntie said. "Because the United States used the Rio Grande during the Civil War, the Anglo and Negro soldiers that passed through saw opportunities—with the Anglos, it was vast land ownership, and with the Negros, freedom from slavery. Mexico offered land, and the only requirement to settlers was to pledge allegiance to Mexico."

"What was wrong with that?" I asked.

Auntie smiled again. "For one thing, once settled, settlers didn't stick to the agreement. For another, grantees didn't fence their lands. It was an honor system of shared grasslands and water. When the Anglos came, they seized the land and built fences."

I didn't know what to say.

I told you about an old Spanish saying, *Con el alambre vino el hambre.* "Yes, you said, 'hunger came with the fencing.'"

We were both quiet for a time. I looked at the wall of pictures displaying an image of the Menger's haunted history, the story of a woman murdered in her room and whose specter sometimes appeared in the main lobby.

"I don't understand," I said, "how could someone just take over the land without any proof of purchase?"

"The grantees only spoke Spanish," Auntie replied. "Most didn't read English. The Anglo had no qualms presenting them with court documents challenging them in an unfamiliar court system with Anglo judges."

"Couldn't they get Anglo lawyers?" I asked.

"Ah, mi Querida," she took in a deep breath. You genuinely don't know anything about bigotry and how it affects the lives of people who are not Anglo.

We passed the restaurant and peered at the menu posted on the door.

"I know where we're going to eat tonight," Auntie grabbed my hand, ending this latest Narciso installment.

"We're going to Mi Tierra's."

I'd lived in San Antonio for nine months during my school year, and Auntie knew of more places than I did.

"My Dirt," I expressed with surprise, "we're going to a restaurant named My Dirt!"

"No, silly, My Land, Mi Tierra means My Land."

"Oh," I answered sheepishly. But it also translated to my dirt, I thought.

★

Mi Tierra was in an area of San Antonio known as El Mercado. I looked across the park from Market Square's entrance and saw the hospital I was taken to when Sister sent me to the emergency room. I didn't realize I'd see it again, and I shuddered.

"What's wrong?" Auntie asked.

"That's the hospital where…that I was taken to, you know, the story I told you when I was so sick," I didn't say anymore, and Auntie took my hand as we walked through what looked and sounded like a Mexican village; Mariachi music played over speakers.

Row after row of long tables displayed Mexican goods, such as peasant dresses, over-the-shoulder shawls, and head coverings known as mantillas. There was a Pharmacia with woodsy, warm spicy, medicinal scents and fragrances. Pinatas of all shapes and sizes hung from the porticos. Hand-painted bean pots, unpolished mortar, and pestle called a molcajete like the one Mama used to make a spicy sauce after plucking the ripe chili petines from the bush growing in our backyard. These sights and smells transported me to the Mexico I visited and to my childhood home in Galveston.

I thought back to the times I'd keep Daddy company at his solitary meal because his workday on the shipping docks ended hours after John's and my early supper. I'd stare at his face as the fiery tiny red peppers, now pico-de-gallo, a mixture of tomatoes, garlic, cilantro, and onion, caused the sweat to pour from his brow and tears to run down his cheeks. I never understood how something so painful could be a pleasure to eat.

¿Quieres probar? he'd ask. Want to taste?

I always said no.

Auntie yanked at my arm and pulled me out of my reverie.

"I'm hungry; let's eat!"

Mi Tierra's entrance had a panadería which greeted us with the delicious aroma of freshly baked bread, pan dulce. The shelves also had Mexican candy with one of my favorites, Leche Quemada.

"I never want to leave this place," I told Auntie. She laughed, and we walked toward the dining room. After our waitress took our order, three Mariachis surrounded us for a song request.

It took little to get Auntie in a playful mood, especially when three handsome young men competed for attention. They only had to make her happy, and she'd provide a generous tip.

"Cancion?" one asked. I noticed that all three ignored me gathering instead around Auntie.

"¿Cómo se llaman? She wanted to know their names. No quick escape for these guys; they would earn their keep.

"Yo soy Francisco," he turned to his companions, "Julian y Antonio."

All three bowed.

"Cántame algo animado." She wanted to hear something lively.

They began with *Nuestros Corazo*nes, "Our Hearts," (by Los Canarios, 1954), a lively piece that made me want to grab one of the guys and polka around the tables. The words made more sense in Spanish but loosely translated to the following:

Our hearts have fallen in love in such a way that neither one nor the other can be happy... It is love love love love love that we feel, it is love love love love... if we love each other. Let us put aside that I do not love you because you do not love me... we do not know our hearts well, that's our fault?

Auntie was most pleased. Our food arrived, and she handed over the bill. It must have been a generous tip because Francisco gazed questioningly at her.

"We'll eat first, then you can sing a couple more," she told them. They politely bowed, and I noticed glances in my direction. I was thrilled.

I inhaled my food, barely saying two words.

"You must have been hungry," Auntie commented. "Starved," I answered.

She looked around for Francisco, Julian, and Antonio and waved to them. They quickly approached our table. I couldn't help thinking that trying to earn a living singing at patrons' tables had to be very chancy. I felt a little sorry for them but overjoyed they would entertain us again.

"¿Otra canción para La Doña? Another song?"

Wow! They were going all out on flattery. They used La Doña as a title of respect for a woman in charge. They were young and cute but not dumb.

"Escoge uno," she allowed them to choose a favorite song.

I covered my mouth with my hands, otherwise, I would have burst out laughing. They sang a rock-and-roll piece, *Agujetas de Color de Rosa*, (Los Hooligans, 1961). This song was about a naïve girl who wore pink but sounded like the English song Itsy Bitsy Yellow Polka Dot Bikini.

★

I floated like I'd had a Margarita, which I didn't. We walked to the end of El Mercado, and I noticed signs indicating historical points of interest. An arrow painted with The Spanish Governor's Mansion marked that it was across the street, one-half block away.

"Auntie, we've got to go see it!" I was excited. "Okay, but what's so special about it?"

"Remember when I told you that Mama registered John and me with the First Families of Bexar County?" Auntie nodded yes.

"Well, that's the mansion of the Viceroyalty of New Spain, José de Urrutia." I pointed to the adobe building now bathed in moonlight. "His daughter married the paymaster, my many great grandfather, Ignacio Inclán.

"Now that's interesting. My Mama Lucia came to San Antonio to meet with Dr. Urrutia, who diagnosed her with terminal cancer. Lucia said she would only trust a relative to examine her. This is more than a coincidence, right?"

"Well, Auntie, you are now getting the opportunity to tour a historical place built by our ancestors."

Auntie looked at me, "The Indians probably built it," she mumbled.

"What?" I responded, "Indians build The Spanish Governor's Mansion?"

"They built all the missions," Auntie responded, "you don't think those aristocratic gentlemen and padres got their fingernails dirty, do you?"

I sighed deeply. I knew nothing about diverse history.

Chapter 14

VAGABONDS AND MALEFACTORS

Auntie walked around the hotel room in a cozy matching three-piece pajama set with a robe, sleeveless t-shirt, and pants. I had received many pajama sets after high school graduation, but nothing like her elegant set.

"Just looking at the picture of Richard King reminded me of my grandfather's mysterious death on his ranch," she told me.

"I never heard that story," I put down Auntie's latest copy of Vogue and straightened up to listen.

"My grandmother, Estefana, was born in 1849 and married Ysidoro Cavazos in 1870. The newlyweds moved to land his father, my great grandfather, granted to him at San Juan de Carricitos and labeled on the 1870 census as porcion 71.

"Oh," I interrupted excitedly. "Guadalupe," I counted on my fingers, "would have been 76 years old. Did, uh, Grandmother Lucia ever tell you her stories?"

Auntie sat at the edge of her bed and looked at me gravely. "No." She then gave her pillow another fluff. I knew the ritual and did the same. She got into bed and smoothed down the covers as if awaiting a breakfast tray.

"The Anglos had a saying when obtaining the land settled by Mexicans, Auntie started dramatically, "'We make deals only with the widow.'"

"That sounds ominous," I responded.

"And it was. Our grandmother, Estefana, became a widow at thirty-seven years of age when our grandfather, Ysidoro, drowned in a pond on the property after he sold a portion of the land."

I opened my mouth in shock, "He was murdered?"

"The Texas Rangers who investigated said it was an accidental drowning."

"But you don't believe it was?"

Auntie shrugged, and I wondered, too, what was the true story.

★

Narciso and Guadalupe sat at each end of the dining table, joined by their lawyer, Señor Rafael De La Garza, and Narciso's oldest son Manuel.

The Cavazos clan now included seven children with the birth of two more boys; Juan Nepomuceno in 1795 and José Maria in 1798. The officials who inspected the progress of the land had left three months ago, and with the year 1799 ending, Narciso would wait no longer to record his wishes and certify his will. He wanted it done before the new century,1800, commenced. His colonists warned him they had seen Americanos on his land, counting the cattle belonging to Narciso and his settlers.

"I know the Americans consider possible vulnerable spots to take as theirs," Narciso remarked, "but our settlement only has a few families, and all must have watchful eyes to guard against foreigners invading our land.

"Papá," Manuel began hesitatingly, but Narciso bellowed loudly.

"Never the Land!" he commanded. "Never sell the land except under dire necessity!"

Narciso was emphatic and kept repeating himself. "Sell the animals to obtain capital if you need immediate funds." He turned to Guadalupe, "Should the need arise for money for the care and support of our children, sell the livestock, understand?"

Guadalupe rose wearily from the table where they'd been sitting for hours. José Maria had fallen asleep, and she placed him on a bed and covered him. Every morning, before the children were awake, she would join the group of women in the community who milked the goats and cows, now doubled in numbers, and pasturing on the rich grassland of the Agostadero. Guadalupe was exhausted.

The casa mayor was the principal house. Surrounding Narciso's and Guadalupe's large one-room log cabin were other cabins, jacales, thatched-roof huts, corrals, chicken coops, and small animal pens. The large patio contained a stone chimney and an open hearth to cook bread. It was also the principal work area for large-scale cooking. Before milking, Guadalupe would place a large cauldron of beans to cook outside.

The patio's roof had a brush cover, shading the home's outdoor kitchen and entrance area during the day's heat. Inside the house, a chopping block stood in the corner for preparing quick meals. The room accommodated a large family with an ample table occupying the center of the room and seating benches. At one end were four beds, two for the boys and two for the girls. Ignacia, now twenty, shared a curtained area with her little sisters. Opposite was Narciso and Guadalupe's bed. Standing against the wall, separating the children's sleeping quarters from the parent's, two large armoires stored bed linens, towels, and the family's modest attire. Narciso's and Guadalupe's youngest, José Maria, continued to share his parent's bed.

Narciso, Señor De La Garza, and Manuel remained at the table discussing the terms of the will. This talk had begun at breakfast, and now was time for the afternoon meal.

Manuel, Narciso's only son with his first wife, Maria Ignacia, was the primary heir to San Juan de Carricitos. Narciso had requested his presence when he discussed the provisions of his will. He knew the burden of losing a parent at an early age. Narciso had been twelve years old when his father died at age thirty-three. In 1799, Narciso was forty-nine years old and wanted his estate in order so nothing would compromise his children's inheritance. His will would include a sitio de Ganado mayor, a league consisting of 4,428 acres for each of his eleven children.

Guadalupe had given Narciso five sons and two daughters. The sons would need a legacy. He and Guadalupe would find suitable partners for their daughters, but he must also consider leaving them plots of land for their dowry. Ignacia had gone from the Agostadero, visiting family in Reynosa, and would return at the end of the month.

Manuel, twenty-eight, pleaded with his father. "Papá, you can realize greater riches by selling the land. Look at what's happening. The Indians are becoming more dangerous, and you must constantly fix the damage they leave behind."

Narciso waved his hand and shakes his head no. He looked at Manuel. To him, the land was tangible evidence that he possessed immense wealth.

"The animals can die, be killed, or be stolen. Drought and a derecho can ruin crops, but the land is forever," he declared forcefully. A derecho, most likely a hurricane, referred to a cluster of thunderstorms traveling in a straight line capable of great destruction.

"Livestock is the livelihood here at San Juan de Carricitos," he looked at the lawyer. "But everyone in the settlement plants corn, beans, squash, chilies, onions, garlic, cilantro, and watermelon near their dwellings. This harvest sustains our community. And even though we have irrigation, farming requires rain from the heavens."

Manuel rose and stood beside Narciso, "I have responsibilities with the Ballí land. I can't manage another large ranch." Manuel had married Pilar, an only child whose parent's land grant was Padre Island.

"They called us 'vagabonds and malefactors,'" Narciso mumbled glumly. "What," Manuel asked. "What did you say?"

Narciso's and Guadalupe's seven children ranged from nine-year-old Jorge, their first, to José María, almost one year old. The other children were four-year-old Juan Nepomuceno, five-year-old José Lino, six-year-old Maria Guadalupe, seven-year-old José Blas, and eight-year-old Clara. Raúl and nine-year-old Jorge were at the pasture tending to the stock.

"Clara," Guadalupe called softly to her eldest daughter sitting in the corner of the room, instructing Maria Guadalupe with an embroidery pattern, "help with dinner."

"José Blas," Guadalupe tapped his shoulder, "go to the larder and get eggs, ham, and cheese." José Blas rose from reading a book.

"José Lino and Maria Guadalupe," Guadalupe whispered, "wash this fruit for our lunch." The children opened the door with the apples and grapes to head to the water well a few steps from the house. "Leave the door open," Guadalupe added quickly. She was never comfortable having the children out of sight.

Guadalupe placed plates and cups on the table, a large pitcher filled with ale and another with milk. She had arranged platters of cold ham, cheese, hard-boiled eggs, sliced bread, cut apples, grapes, and a bowl each of figs and pecans in less than an hour. She kept a small pot of beans and corn tortillas warming at the hearth and passed steaming bowls to each one at the table.

The family usually had their large dinner around this time. Later, at dusk, Guadalupe served a lighter meal consisting of chocolate, a Mexican hot drink blended with toasted cacao grounded with almonds, sugar, cinnamon, vanilla, or nutmeg, accompanied with empanadas, a Mexican sweet bread stuffed with Guadalupe's fig preserves. The men looked at Guadalupe, and Narciso praised her for quickly putting together this meal.

The men reached for a plump fig, each heavy with its syrupy liqueur, which drizzled down Narciso's chin. He licked his fingertips and said, "…a subtle hint of honey and berries, right?" Figs were brought from the Mediterranean region of Spain to Texas by the conquistador Escandon who scattered seedlings when he scouted the area in 1520.

Manuel rose from the table and stood next to his father. "Who called you a vagabond and malefactor?" he asked Narciso.

Narciso was quiet for a few minutes. He took a long swig of his drink and pulled back from the bench, sighing deeply.

"The Royal inspectors came late. This past summer, they checked on the progress of San Juan de Carricitos." He turned to Manuel, "You remember that the community must prosper within five years of settlement?"

Manuel nodded and replied slowly, "I can see it's showing promise."

Narciso looked at Manuel, then at Señor De La Garza. "I chose a group of families from the more established ranchos to spend time with the inspectors, you know, take them around their cabins, show them their ranchos, their crop, the animals." He rose and stood infront of the opened door.

"We were expecting two, maybe three inspectors. We even put together two jacales for their privacy."

"I can understand how they wouldn't be happy with the accommodations; those men have palaces in Monterrey. …and their evaluation?" Manual asked.

"We dressed for the occasion. We wanted the inspectors to know we came from nobility. Yes, I failed in keeping with the agreement, but Indians had driven off some of the families that came with us. The inspectors were unimpressed with our progress. They said I did not meet the expectations required by the government."

"Did you get their report?" Señor De La Garza asked. "Can I see it?"

Narciso turned from the doorway to the armoire that contained essential papers, handed them over, and then sat at the table.

Señor De La Garza read the document. "It describes the inhabitants of San Juan de Carricitos as 'vagabonds and malefactors,'" he said out loud and looked at Narciso with raised eyebrows.

"Continue reading," Narciso encouraged.

"'…and although dressed in luxury, were lazy, cringing, and fearful whiners.'"

"Dressed in luxury," Narciso snickered, "I wore a twenty-year-old evening suit at the dinner Guadalupe prepared in their honor.

Guadalupe wore her newest dress—the one she wore at our wedding six years ago."

"What was their contention?" Manuel couldn't understand why the evaluation was so brutal.

"We wanted the inspectors to understand that we alone launched San Juan de Carricitos." Narciso continued. "We had no help from Mexico or Spain, and no military is close enough to protect us against the Indian attacks."

"But…?" Manuel wanted more answers.

"We have no church, I haven't begun building the main house, the Hacienda, and they considered the town square too crude because the floor is packed dirt, not flagstone. They didn't accept our complaints that the Apache set this community back by destroying the crop, burning our huts, and killing the animals."

Narciso slumped over the table.

A few minutes later, he resumed. "I must finish the Hacienda quickly.

This cabin we're in must become a community center. Those inspectors talked out of both sides of their mouths. However, they accused me of not living up to my commitment to Christianize the Karankawa Indians, and I don't know if they'd approve or deny the settlement. It's been thirty years since Mexico provided resources to build a mission, must less a military post. I, the grantee, am solely responsible for protecting my property as reciprocity for the free lands."

"Papá," Manuel drew close to Narciso to encourage him, "you must sell some of the lands."

"I agree," Señor De La Garza butted in, "Mexico seeks to strengthen its borders through colonization laws. When that happens, you may have squatters and Americans who take what they want. Without constant patrolling, you won't even know they've intruded, then five years later, they can claim themselves as homesteaders."

"That can't happen," Narciso said firmly, "I have the official document from the King of Spain giving me this land."

Señor De La Garza placed his hand on Narciso's shoulder. "Narciso, the tide for revolution escalates. Both the Mexican upper class and Americans compete directly with Mexican enterprises. These men will go to war before they allow Americanos to take over their industries in Mexico, and the Americanos will too."

Narciso stared hard at Señor De La Garza, who bravely continued.

"You're not in the heat of the fight—yet. I'm in Laredo, and we have a garrison that protects us. You're up against fierce competitors, Narciso, who don't always play fair. These people would like nothing better than to deal with Guadalupe, the widow, easily bullied to sell cheap." He looked over at Guadalupe, who pursed her lips and sat rigidly straight in her chair. "With her living here in the middle of nowhere, what do you think will happen if you have an accident and die?" He stopped to look at Narciso, who glared back, impervious to the 'what ifs.'

"The Americans," Señor De La Garza continued, "have their hands everywhere in Texas, and the Rio Grande allows them to trade with the Mexican elites and the French."

French products were considered superior to those from Spain and Mexico, creating competition for French goods. Mexican elites and Americans would trade amongst themselves and with the Indians.

Señor De La Garza again looked at the document. "It says that the 601,657 acres of land granted was for a Hacienda, a large estate."

"Just before the inspectors came," Narciso responded, "four tribes combined and assaulted the property. I later learned they were a group of Apache, Comanches, Mescaleros, and Kickapoo. They ransacked, burned the shelters, looted the stored dry goods, and stole the yearlings we'd corral for training. Do you know how long it took to rebuild?"

Señor De La Garza looked at Narciso and back to the document. "You complained to the inspectors that the Indians drove off the original families."

"Well, yes," Narciso responded, "Five families that initially came with me didn't remain after the third attack. That was a huge loss for the community."

Señor De La Garza again looked at the document. "They wrote that you said those who returned to Mexico didn't abandon the land."

"It was my land," Narciso stood up and lightly pounded a fist to his chest. "How could the land be abandoned when it was mine? People desert their land; it comes back to me."

"And" the attorney continued reading, "the inspectors concluded that because of the large concession of land, you should have given priority to secure the settlement against the Indian invasion."

"I agreed to collaborate with the Indians, not fight them," Narciso responded heatedly, "I never expected a constant state of conflict."

The men remained silent. Manuel moved toward his father, who raised a hand for him to stop.

"Now, let's finalize this will. What else? Oh yes, I've doubled my branded stock and, in addition, now have 6,400 sheep and 5,000 unbranded cattle." He looked at the faces of those seated, including Guadalupe's.

"The land will never be for sale, is that understood?"

Chapter 15

SPIRITS OF SAN ANTONIO

Auntie wanted to visit the Alamo. "I never took the time on my own to visit this famous landmark," she turned to look at me. Our ancestor, Juan Seguin, was a signer of the Texas Declaration of Independence and was good friends with Stephen F. Austin."

"I had no idea," I responded, having lost count of the number of ancestors I'd learned about on this trip. "Our forebears got around, didn't they?" I responded.

Auntie laughed, "And they did all their travels on horseback or wagons."

"Who even thinks about pioneer travels?" I thought. "I got to learn history in Auntie's eye-popping GTO."

We exited the hotel, and I asked Auntie, "Want to go to the Alamo using the Riverwalk?" The Riverwalk was below street level.

Auntie looked a little confused. "It's just around the corner from here," she said.

Sure enough, the Alamo was maybe several hundred steps from the Menger. I was so used to riding in a car and Auntie driving miles and miles to destinations that I'd lost any concept of distance.

According to the pamphlet we picked up at the hotel, the Missions—

Espada, San Juan, and San José—were undergoing some level of restoration, except Concepción, whose renovation was complete. Also mentioned were the renovations to the original estuaries, acequias, other irrigation resources, agricultural fields, and the aqueduct at Mission Espada.

Auntie explained the differences, "Estuaries are the surrounding wetlands or bodies of water found where rivers meet the sea. Acequias, on the other hand, were man-made to control water distribution and allocation."

Auntie's stories about Narciso, a bona fide pioneer, made me more aware of my roots.

During my second semester of college, I learned about my paternal connection to San Antonio. My high school guidance counselor suggested I apply to Incarnate Word College (IWC), and in the Fall of 1966, I began freshman year. My brother John had done the research for a college project and discovered the Inclan name among the list of the Canary Islanders who were the First Families of Bexar County. Mama submitted nine generations of genealogical paperwork, and Johnny and I received official documents naming us as descendants. However, it was only by coincidence that I'd chosen Incarnate Word College. Mama had wanted me nearby in Houston; I wanted San Antonio for no other reason but for being further away from Galveston.

This time I would use the Mission Trail to study the landscape. The Alamo wasn't isolated like the other Missions ten miles away and appeared out of place compared to the tall buildings and busy restaurants surrounding it. However, the large anteroom had documents, pictures, and artifacts that conveyed its sacred history and greatness. I walked out to the enclosed garden, hoping to conjure images of its earlier time. I read from the pamphlet that in the 1500s, this first San Antonio mission was built in a remote spot near the San Antonio River when Cabeza de Vaca first documented it during his explorations of Texas. I remembered the other four Missions were two to three miles apart. It would take all day if we wanted to visit all the Missions.

"We'd better get going if we're to tour the rest of the Missions," I told

Auntie. Now that I was more acquainted with the history, I wanted to experience the missions as historical venues and as sacred places echoing the spirits of the past. I also hoped to sense what life must have felt like. I wanted to walk the Mission grounds to glimpse what estuaries and acequias would have looked like on Narciso's fields at the Agostadero.

Heading back to the hotel, Auntie commented, "The pamphlet says there's a campaign in progress to have the missions ready for the 1968 San Antonio World's Fair,"

"It's all over the newspapers," I said, "they're calling it HemisFair."

"HemisFair, what a great name," Auntie sounded intrigued. "I may have to come back next year to spend time in San Antonio."

"I'll be here for at least three more years," I quickly added. "San Antonio celebrates 250 years of its founding in…" I looked down at the pamphlet, "1718."

Auntie read more.

"The fair's theme, Confluence of Civilizations in the Americas, will celebrate the various ethnic groups. That sounds really interesting," Auntie said. "Texas has been under six flags," she hesitated and looked up, "and I can name them; Spain, France, the Republic of Mexico, the Republic of Texas, the Confederate States, and the United States." I smiled and said, "Bravo," clapping my hands. I was too embarrassed to confess that I thought Six Flags over Texas was merely the signature tune for the theme park of the same name that opened in Arlington, Texas.

"Let's get a bite to eat," Auntie looked at me before starting up the engine. "Any suggestions?"

"The only restaurant I know is Earl Ables, across the street from The Word." I'd only completed one year at IWC and had a part-time job on campus, so I hadn't had time to familiarize myself with the city.

Auntie turned onto Broadway, which took us to the restaurant's location, catty-corner to The Word. We were seated immediately. Auntie looked around and commented, "This place reminds me of the restaurants in

New York City. I hope the food is as good."

"Mama talked about New York City when during the depression, Grandmother Lucia took her, Aunt Genevieve, and Uncle Alex. You and Uncle Diaz owned and managed a brownstone in Greenwich Village. Right?" Auntie looked up from the menu and nodded. I continued, "Grandmother Lucia kept up the apartment, and her children took on jobs." I looked at Auntie to confirm Mama's story. "Mama loved her life in New York City. She worked in a laundry, Aunt Genevieve at Woolworths, and Uncle Alex sold newspapers in the morning and shined shoes in the afternoons." Auntie just nodded. I suddenly remembered her painful memories of New York City. We talked about them early in our trip.

"I've only been to this restaurant once," I quickly changed the subject. "One-night last Fall, a group of us decided at eleven o'clock we were hungry. On Fridays, our curfew was midnight, so we had plenty of time."

Auntie stared at the menu's extensive selection and decided on fried chicken. I ordered a turkey sandwich with fries.

"At The Word, we got three meals a day," I began talking on campus life, "Sister Xavier, the cafeteria proctor, had a motto: 'We're here to feed, not to fatten.'" We both laughed. "The menus were good and filling. I worked in the cafeteria and saw how the chef prepared the food."

Our plates came, and we both were quiet until we finished eating.

"Well," Auntie said and turned to ask the waitress for the dessert menu, "Food should be enjoyed." She looked and ordered a chocolate black bottom slice of pie. She handed me the menu, "Get something."

"I'll just have a taste of yours," I said.

Auntie shrugged, "Okay, but you only live once."

★

I waved my hand toward the park across the street outside Earl Ables.

"Auntie, that's Brackenridge Park." She shielded her eyes to look.

"What's there?" she asked with interest.

"It's a San Antonio landmark and includes a stretch of the San Antonio River, the Japanese Tea Garden, and the Sunken Garden, an outdoor theatre."

"How did it come to be here?" Auntie looked around the busy Broadway street.

"From what I learned of The Word's history, Colonel Brackenridge owned 500 acres of this land," I made a circle to include the spot we stood on outside the restaurant. "He sold his house and a couple of hundred acres to the Sisters of the Incarnate Word. The nuns first built a college prep boarding school, then the college," I pointed to The Word at the corner of Broadway and Hildebrand streets. "Just across is Brackenridge Park, opened to the public."

Auntie appeared interested, so I continued. "Both the park and The Word's campus are spectacular." I looked at Auntie. "The areas are covered with massive pecan trees. I loved studying under those trees."

Auntie smiled and nodded.

"You can't see it from here, but an immense swimming pool...," I pointed in its direction, "in a more secluded section, stays full of sparkling water from an underwater spring. Whenever we dorm girls sunbathed on the weekend, helicopters from nearby Ft. Sam Houston kept noisy surveillance over us."

Auntie laughed joyously, "Young people having fun. That's how it should be."

"I do enjoy living on campus," I told Auntie. She squeezed me against her.

"The best thing about Brackenridge Park," I said, "is you can walk through it at any time of the day or night."

"What would you be doing walking through the park at night?" Auntie covered her mouth with her palm, her eyes wide and glaring.

The park was less than half a mile from the dorm, but as you crossed the street, trees comprised a wooded area by the college. "One of the girls wanted a der Wienerschnitzel," I pointed to the small hot dog building directly in front of the park's entrance, "and a group of us accompanied her."

"Oh, my goodness, Querida, didn't you realize how dangerous that was?"

I just blinked. I wouldn't tell Auntie that we'd all come in pajamas, too. And the danger was not on our minds when we walked through a forest-like park in the dead of night. The all-girls school didn't allow pants, so whenever worn, we had to put on a trench-coat coverup, which we donned over our pajamas while strolling through the woods.

Auntie drove the short distance to the Brackenridge Park entrance and parked. As we exited the car, I remembered, "There's also horseback riding."

Auntie stopped, "I love horseback riding. Want to do that?" I blinked, "I've never been."

"Why not? Horses are in your genes," Auntie said in mock shock, "think about Narciso and his herd of horses…and Haro."

I admitted that I liked Haro and quickly absolved his contrary personality.

We followed the signs to the stables, and I felt excited about riding a horse.

"This will be a better way to see the park, you'll see," Auntie said excitedly.

"We're both in dresses," I reminded her. "My shoes are fine, but yours are a bit glamorous." I referred to her high heels.

"I'm sure they will have stuff we can buy," Auntie responded.

I had never owned pants, much less a pair of blue jeans, and began to join in Auntie's excitement.

We entered a small building that smelled of polished leather, and Auntie approached the counter. A friendly man welcomed us warmly.

"You ladies come to ride horses?" he asked.

"Yes, sir," Auntie replied, ready to start her playful banter. "However, as you can see, we didn't come prepared to ride; any suggestions?"

"Yes, ma'am," he responded enthusiastically, "we have everything here; cowboy hats, boots, chaps, and, of course," he opened the door to a back room, "blue jeans and cowboy shirts. If you need help, holler for Tom."

Auntie turned to me. "You ready to ride?" I nodded yes.

"You'll find everything you need there," he told us as we entered the room. "The dressing room is right there," he pointed to the curtained booth with a mirror. I had no idea how to determine the pants size, so I first looked at the tops and decided on a Brackenridge Park t-shirt. Auntie went directly to her size.

"Are you going to pick jeans," Auntie asked as she tucked in a blue gingham cowboy shirt. I really did like the idea of a pair of blue jeans.

"I'm not sure where to start; I've never worn jeans, and I sew all my dresses."

Auntie asked how I picked the sizes on my patterns. I told her that I was a size five based on the measurements. She looked at the shelves marked with the sizes and pulled out a pair. "Oh," I said meekly, "I didn't know the sizes were the same as on the patterns I sew." When I slipped on the pants, they fit perfectly. I tucked in my T- shirt.

"Now for the boots!" Auntie was going all Western. She stepped out from the dressing area and hollered for Tim, who happily brought out an array. Auntie picked a pair and tucked in her pant legs as she slid on the boots." She also asked if I wanted a pair, but I nodded no. I only wore specific shoe brands due to my numerous foot surgeries. Boots reminded me too much of casts and braces.

Another man greeted us at the counter.

"I'm the stable master, George; how are you ladies doing?"

"Ready to ride," Auntie replied enthusiastically. Auntie looked great, and she knew it! Now, she needed a cowboy hat but didn't seem interested when Tom asked if she wanted to try some on.

"How familiar are you with riding?" George asked as he turned to Auntie, then me.

"I rode all the time when I was young, but this is my niece's first time."

George nodded. "I need to know your level of experience. All our horses are safe and great with riders, but I will give the young lady a truly gentle one."

We walked out a back door to a stable entrance that smelled of hay and manure.

"Y'all wait here, and I'll get the horses," George said.

My heart was beating faster, and my hands were sweaty. Auntie looked around and babbled something about the park's beauty. I barely heard what she said.

George came out with two horses. One was completely brown, and the other was black and white, spotted with a black mane and tail. I slowly turned my head up. Both horses looked huge.

He handed Auntie the reins to the brown one. "This is Sadie." Auntie rubbed the horse's head, "Hi, Sadie." The horse snorted.

He walked the other horse to me and handed me the reins. "This is Spirit, and she's so gentle I'd trust her with my three-year-old son."

I followed Auntie's example, patted her quickly on the nose, and greeted her with "Hi, Spirit." Spirit didn't respond, and my stomach muscles tightened even more.

"The horses know the trail," George said, "the trail rounds the park, then brings you back here. You'll be going around a lake that feeds from the San Antonio River. Sadie and Spirit are well-acquainted with tourists. Take your time and enjoy the ride, which should take about an hour." He patted Sadie standing next to him.

George first helped Auntie onto Sadie, then me with Spirit. "Just give a little shove against her, and she'll get going."

Auntie followed George's instructions, and off Sadie went. "See you soon," Auntie waved to George as Sadie followed the graveled trail.

Spirit just stood there. I was afraid to poke her too hard and gently tapped her again with my foot. She did nothing. She appeared to be concentrating on chewing, so George spoke quietly in her ear.

Spirit snorted and began slowly walking. She stopped, turned her head, and looked at George.

"Jiggle your reins, and she'll get moving," he told me. I did. She moved slowly, and I mean slow. Then bit by bit began following the trail that Auntie was on. At least, I hoped that was what she was doing. Auntie was nowhere in sight.

The narrow gravel trail twisted and turned. Bushes, small blooming trees, and cacti were on both sides of the path. It was a most solitary ride, and after fifteen minutes, I called out to Auntie. No answer. I then noticed Spirit veering onto a winding dirt path in an even more heavily wooded area. I wondered if we were still on the familiar trail George had mentioned. Still no sight of Auntie. Spirit must be lost, and I began panicking. I thought about San Juan de Carricitos and calmed myself, thinking that this must be how it felt to be in the vast woodlands of the Agostadero. The only noises were of Spirit's slow clomping and the birds' loud chirping as if trying to warn me of something. Once again, my stomach tightened. Why hasn't Auntie come looking for me? Then, Spirit stopped in her tracks.

She refused to move, and when I shook the reins, she turned her head in my direction and bared her teeth. She made a sound like a guttural growl. I froze. Then, after what seemed like minutes passing, I threw the reins down, raised my hands, and said aloud,

"Okay, Spirit, you're the boss."

Spirit then showed me a side of her that George didn't seem to know.

First, she went off the paved path and through the brush. I was flailing my arms to protect my face from slapping branches and scratching my face and arms. She then stopped in the middle of a large bush that, I was sure, covered us from view. I was sputtering and spitting out branches and leaves from my mouth and nose. We were near the river, and, without warning, she dove in, creating a huge splash, stopped, and remained rooted like a statue. I was drenched in my new clothes, threw off the reins, and clung to her neck.

"I've been looking for you; what are you doing there?" Auntie yelled from the opposite side of the river. "The trail circles around." She began to laugh.

"Spirit decided on a shortcut," I sputtered, trying my hand at humor when I just wanted to cry. I knew why I was nervous about horses. Whenever my dorm mates made plans to go horseback riding, I never accompanied them, using my academic workload as an excuse.

"Loosen your hold on her neck; maybe you're choking her," Auntie giggled.

"I have no choice but to wait for this horse to decide what she's going to do with me next," I hollered back, sniffling. "I don't swim."

"The river is probably only knee-deep," Auntie responded, laughing heartily.

"I don't care," I answered back, "she knows she's got the best of me. If I get off now, she'll probably kick me."

"Will you be okay if I go get George?"

"Yes," I answered, and Auntie left, a trail of giggles following in her tracks.

Sadie and Auntie arrived with George, also on a horse. Auntie made no effort to hide her amusement. George, on the other hand, was stunned.

"Spirit," George yelled, "get out of there right now!"

Spirit turned her head and snorted. I was too afraid to loosen my grip on her neck, and I didn't want to see her substantial bare teeth again, so I buried my face in her mane.

"Spirit!" George yelled again, this time with a tone of anger.

Spirit had been standing in the soft river sediment for several minutes. I envisioned her feet embedded, and she'd need to buck to get out. That meant I could still end up in the water with Spirit's hoofs stomping me to oblivion.

George maneuvered his horse into the river and picked up the loose reins. I heard him quietly scolding Spirit and Spirit snorting back as if explaining herself. She did a little wiggle and a waddle, getting out of the water. I was right—her hooves had been firmly planted, but she didn't buck. When we returned to the stables, George helped me off the horse, apologizing profusely. Auntie, still laughing, got off Sadie and said, "Your first encounter with a horse that has the personality of Haro." I glared at her, which didn't faze her in the least.

Tim came rushing out of the shop, and I could see he was upset. He took Auntie aside, but I was humiliated and rushed inside to change out of my wet clothes. When I came out of the dressing room, Tim took my soaked garments and placed them into a plastic bag. "You can have the hotel launder these for you," he said sheepishly, looking over at Auntie. She gave him a big smile and took the bag from his hands.

"What an exciting day," she said, high stepping in her new gear as we headed to the car. Tim wouldn't let me pay for your clothes or our rides." She was as chipper as a schoolgirl.

I didn't respond. I then thought about the other embarrassing moments we'd encountered on this trip; when Auntie's drawers dropped while dancing and a cow greeted me in the outdoor toilet. Auntie wouldn't let anything spoil the day, so I mellowed my mood, "Thank you for everything. I'm glad you didn't have to pay for my clothes."

She took a breath to reply, hesitated, then said, "Still want to go to the Missions?"

"No, I need a shower." I wanted to wash my hair and recover from the horseback riding fiasco. I was no longer in the mood to follow the trail of the Missions that would involve a lot of driving from one to the other and more walking. We sat on a nearby bench in the park for several minutes, mesmerized by the stillness. In the distance, we could hear cars passing by on Broadway. Above us, birds were chirping and fluttering.

Auntie looked up at the birds. "They're trying to get the kids to settle down," Auntie said jokingly, attempting to break my glum mood.

We were quiet for several minutes, then Auntie asked, "Had enough excitement for the day?" I nodded.

"I think it's time for both of us to return home. I still have to drive to California after I drop you off," Auntie said and smiled.

"I know, I wish I was going to California with you," I lamented.

"Next year, we'll do another trip. I'll pick you up, and we can do HemisFair together. Then I'll show you all the places I lived in as a child—Runge, New Braunfels, Goliad, and Lockhart." She looked at my downcast face and smiled. I smiled back.

"You good with all that," she asked, again looking at my reaction.

"I'm good," I answered, "I'll have something to look forward to next summer.

"That's settled," we rose and headed to the car.

Auntie ordered our dinner from Menger's restaurant; we sat around the service cart and ate—me in the hotel's bathrobe and a towel wrapped around my head; Auntie was still in her riding gear. She looked good in those tight jeans and a Western shirt.

We performed our nightly wash-up ritual and climbed into our beds.

"I really want to know for how long San Juan de Carricitos existed". I scooted under the covers and leaned against the pillow propped against the headboard.

Auntie began, "I may not have this right, but this is what I believe happened."

Chapter 16

TIME TO SAY GOODBYE

Minutes before 1802 peeked from a moonlit sky, Narciso, Guadalupe, and the surrounding community of families gathered the effigies they had scattered across the property. They built a bonfire and, as the clock neared midnight, began burning these images to obliterate the suffering of the old year. These ficticios and espantapájar, were dummies and scarecrows stuffed with tree bark, wood chips, pine straw, moss, grass clippings, or leaves—refuse from constructing the Agostadero de San Juan de Carricitos.

The year 1801 had been merciless. Anything that could have gone wrong had gone wrong. The Agostadero needed more families, and because of that year's extreme hardship, some of the original members returned to their origins in Nuevo Leon. It felt as if it didn't matter how hard they worked; the Indians appeared more aggressive and no longer hid in the shadows of trees and bushes.

Narciso saw them in the distance atop horses, arrogant and proud, after an especially tortuous night of burning and pillaging. The squandering of their lands enraged the Indians, and the tribes united; Apache, Comanche, and Kickapoo, a migratory group who typically set up posts near other Indian villages. They came in bands to wipe out the whites to stop them from stealing their lands, decimating their food, and taking their women as wives and mistresses. Narciso had word that their meat supply had dwindled as more white men moved into their lands, slaughtering game indiscriminately and leaving the carcass to rot because the animal hide was the more valuable commodity.

Narciso felt he'd embraced the Indians into the Agostadero, and he didn't consider them a lower class of citizenry, as most elites treated them in Mexico.

"Didn't I welcome and respect the Indians living on my grandfather's Hacienda?" he'd say to Guadalupe.

The Indians living on La Hacienda De Los Cavazos in Nuevo Leon were probably descendants of the Tlaxcalans. When Hernán Cortés encountered the Tlaxcalans kingdom in 1519, he observed a monarchy of royals, princes, princesses, and fierce warriors. During Moctezuma's reign, the Tlaxcalans lived in mortal danger, with their men, women, and children kidnapped and enslaved, some for sacrifice to the Aztec gods. Cortés respected the Tlaxcalans' hard-earned sovereignty fighting the Aztecs. If they united with the Spaniards to destroy their rival, Moctezuma, Emperor of the Aztecs, Cortés promised them their continued independence. In 1521, the warriors did fight mightily against the Aztecs, and Cortés granted the Tlaxcalans benefits no other tribe obtained. They would keep their lands in perpetuity. Allowed to carry arms to defend themselves, the Spanish gave the Tlaxcalans saddles, spurs, and armor for themselves and their horses to protect them in battle. The Tlaxcalans' cunning and warring mastery gave Hernán Cortés the military strength to destroy Moctezuma.

Cortés arranged marriages between his closest lieutenants and the royal princesses after baptizing the women and giving them Christian names. The Spanish saw their culture as superior, so any mestizo children from these unions were sent away to be raised by a proper Spanish family. In time, the two cultures blended and blurred. After almost 300 years of peace with the Indians of Mexico, the survival of the San Juan de Carricitos community depended upon fighting the Indians of Tejas.

At 52 years old, Narciso had been taming the Agostadero for almost nine years. He still needed more time to complete the pledge he'd given to Spain and Mexico to establish a township. As of now, his community was still a hamlet because of the scarcity of pioneers.

Mexico remained in a constant state of conflict; first, with the elites, Spaniards who held titles, wealth, and influence, and the criollos, who, like Narciso, had been born in Mexico from parents who were Spaniards but were only allowed secondary roles in governance. Those of Spanish fathers and Indian mothers, the mestizos, the non-elites, the peones, began to resist the tyranny the elite groups had imposed. This conjoining of strong cultures, Spanish and Indian, created an ethnic group who wanted their rightful piece of the land and riches the elites had taken from their ancestors.

Spain, constantly at war with Great Britain, France, and the Portuguese, demanded more wealth from Mexico, which struggled to maintain the leadership and control of its inhabitants. Mexico's elites had property, wealth, and voice. Narciso was left to fend for himself to the struggles and conflict of a new frontier—one Mexico wanted to maintain but didn't have the forces or the inclination to help. The arrogant elites who lived in grand haciendas in Monterrey came to the Agostadero to inspect Narciso's progress and diminished his struggle blaming his aristocratic pedigree for the lack of improvement at San Juan de Carricitos. They had called him a crook and a vagrant. They claimed that Narciso did not have the cojones to establish a community.

"You're not dirtying your blue-blooded hands, and that's why you haven't fulfilled your pledge," the inspector from Monterrey had scoffed. Never mind that these government agents were the ones who had ensnared the Indians who built their wealth, while Narciso was left to personal resources.

"I don't care how long it takes to make a township," Narciso repeated to Guadalupe, "but I must be left in peace."

His family was growing, although still too young to work on the land. His older brothers had told him they savored becoming Hacienda landowners in Texas. La Hacienda De Los Cavazos in Mexico would never belong to anyone but their eldest brother, José Nazario, and his heirs. José Manuel and Francisco came with their families and joined the community at the Agostadero.

But Narciso's aches and pains had physically handicapped him. His legs bowed, and he shuffled back and forth with a pronounced limp. Several nights a week, in an unoccupied jacala, Guadalupe would pour him a steaming bath where Narciso would soak amidst the calming scents of rosemary and rose petals. She'd brew him a drink of datura, datura stramonium, a plant the Aztecs had discovered to relieve pain. When his knees were especially inflamed, she'd apply atropine, the pain-relieving chemical in datura that absorbed through the skin. She also cooked with spicy chiles, known for their analgesic properties.

One day, Raúl told Narciso that he would soon leave the Agostadero for Mexico—his elderly mother was ailing, and he was her eldest son. Narciso alone would have to finish making San Juan de Carricitos a Spanish Mexican Texas town with a grand hacienda.

"You're my oldest friend," Narciso looked woefully at Raúl, who turned his face to evade his best friend's anguish.

Soon after, Narciso had to face another difficult decision and acknowledge that Haro stayed alive because of him. The stallion had been his companion since Narciso's twenty-first birthday, and Narciso could not imagine putting him down.

"He's never going to leave you as long as you continue to sleep with him every night," Guadalupe gently admonished. "You can barely walk, and that hard, cold ground you lie on doesn't help with your inflamed knees."

Raúl had also spoken with Narciso, "Haro has terrible eyesight; look at his coat, Narciso," the once glistening black coat was now grey and mottled with patches of dry skin. "He's 32 years old and has lived longer than most horses."

"He insists on joining me when we go to the pasture," Narciso defended, "it's his sanctuary."

"Yes, but he lags far behind Allegria," Narciso's mare. "What would happen if he fell and couldn't get back up? He'd die all alone." Raúl tried to reason.

Narciso snapped, "He hasn't fallen yet, but I wait beside him when he has to rest until he recovers enough to continue."

"Yes, "Raúl persisted, "and sometimes he turns back to the ranch limping. Like you, Narciso, he's in pain."

Narciso replied softly, "I know. I know. But I can't let him go. Not yet."

Raúl wouldn't let up. He'd be leaving soon and wanted to be with Narciso when Haro was laid to rest.

"Narciso," Raúl placed his hand on Narciso's shoulder, "Look at what he does when you barricade him in his stall. He groans and nickers until you come to stay by his side. He doesn't want you out of his sight. For God's sake, Narciso, he won't even eat unless you watch him."

"I've been letting the community down, taking so much time nursing Haro. But he's not an ordinary horse. I have to know when he's ready, and I'm not sure he is."

Even though Haro was nothing but trouble to anyone charged with his care, people knew Narciso's struggle was due to his deep love for this contrary horse. The ranchers watched as Haro declined further. Haro had annoyed Raúl from the time he was a yearling, but on his last day, Raúl took loving care of this beloved stallion. First, he gently coaxed him into drinking a calming blend, which Raúl dared to place into Haro's mouth while Narciso stroked his forehead, which enabled Haro to fall asleep.

Narciso buried Haro on the grounds at San Juan de Carricitos. A week later, Raúl left for his mother's home in Mexico. Narciso was now without either of his closest companions, Raúl or Haro. Guadalupe understood his period of sorrow.

★

Ignacia returned all aglow from her extended visit to Nuevo Leon, Mexico. She had met a third cousin, once removed, Maximino Cavazos Gutierrez, and they were in love. Narciso approved of the union; after all, he was a Cavazos. The families began communications for a wedding in Mexico. There was no grand hacienda at San Juan de Carricitos, which lacked an appropriate place for a wedding set for August.

"The dowry will keep the family close," Narciso told Guadalupe. "I'm also giving them 100 heads of unbranded cattle."

Since Ignacia's mother was deceased and Guadalupe was busy with el Agostadero and young children, Ignacia planned frequent trips to Mexico.

The wedding day arrived, filling the family with joy and excitement. Narciso and Guadalupe traveled with their young children to Narciso's former home at La Hacienda. Ignacia's married sisters, Maria de Los Santos, and Francesca were bridesmaids; her brother Manuel, a groomsman. The younger Cavazos,' also attendants, included three-year-old José María, the ring bearer.

When Narciso walked his daughter down the aisle, he couldn't help but think about the pomp of his wedding day to Maria Ignacia. "That was 32 years ago," he thought. Theirs' had been an extravagant wedding in Nuevo Leon. Ignacia copied the old traditions of her mother's wedding day, beginning with selecting Padrinos, godparents who contributed to the expenses of the wedding.

Maria de Los Santos, the eldest sister, was the matron of honor. She provided two wine glasses for the toast, a guestbook, the prayer book, and the rosary from Ignacia's first communion. Maria de Los Santos had safeguarded the family's kneeling pillow their mother had used on her wedding day for Ignacia's. At the altar, Narciso turned to face Ignacia, a stunning replica of her mother in the dress worn by Maria Ignacia on her wedding day. They embraced, and their eyes filled with tears. He then placed Ignacia's hand into Maximino's and returned to Guadalupe's side, wiping his face with calloused fingers.

The bishop began by blessing an ornamental box filled with thirteen coins, the "arras." The box represented good wishes and prosperity; the coins represented Christ and his twelve apostles. The best man assumed charge of the box and returned it to the bishop at the end of the ceremony. Then Ignacia accepted the gift and promised to trust Maximino with managing financial decisions. The couple repeated their vows, after which the Padrinos de Lazo placed a large loop of orange blossoms around their necks in the shape of an eight. They wore the Lazo throughout the service as a symbol of binding love and shared obligations. With the religious ceremony complete, the celebration, lasting for two days, moved to a grand salon with food, musicians, and dancing. The home where Narciso resided with Maria Ignacia and later with Guadalupe was still unoccupied, and the family stayed there during their visit.

Guadalupe and Narciso took the time to walk around Ojo de Agua, where they had often met secretly; Guadalupe's arm looped into Narciso's. They spoke of their happiness and the joyous wedding.

"I would never have gotten this far without you," he said to Guadalupe. "My dreams may have never been realized."

Guadalupe pressed close to Narciso and lowered her eyes. "You offered me a life I never imagined," she responded.

They passed their favorite hiding place, underneath the massive leaves of the Montezuma Bald Cypress tree and detected a soft giggle. They looked at each other, moved quickly away, then laughed heartily at what they knew was happening.

Upon returning to San Juan de Carricitos, they resolved to accomplish every requirement to upgrade and safeguard the land. It was time to finalize the pledge with Spain. Two months after the wedding, after a four-year lapse, Guadalupe suspected that she was once again pregnant. "We'll have a new baby in the new year." The baby was due around February 1803.

★

Narciso had an idea for the upcoming New Year's Eve and wanted to celebrate with the families he and Guadalupe had become so close to while building San Juan de Carricitos.

"We must have a great feast on Nochevieja," he suggested to Guadalupe. "As dawn begins to appear," he dramatically looked up and raised his hands, extending his fingers, "we'll bring out pambazos, (a thick Mexican bread), tortillas, chorizo, chicken—a feast." Guadalupe laughed in delight; as the Doña in charge of community events, she agreed with Narciso. She knew just how she'd make the celebration festive. Even though heavily pregnant, she counted on the women of the community, who helped one another to accomplish goals, provide meals, and watch over the children.

The wedding had boosted Narciso's spirits to the point that he earnestly engaged in working the ranch. The community needed another well, and Narciso brought hope to the pioneers and found the appropriate spot to dig for water.

Then, a smallpox scourge infested the community, and on November 2, Narciso's brother, Juan Francisco, succumbed to the disease. His brother was fifty-five years old.

Later that same month, Narciso received a message that his oldest daughter, Maria de Los Santos, had died at thirty-three. Narciso was inconsolable. "She was fine three months ago, he wailed to Guadalupe, who felt that this death, the worst of all possible news, would destroy Narciso.

Guadalupe, now in her last stages of pregnancy, tried to console her husband. She believed with all the death surrounding him; he had suffered a broken heart. She watched his decline; poor appetite, trouble sleeping, and he'd developed a deep cough. Just yesterday, a group of vaqueros carried him into the house after he had collapsed while digging a trench.

Her overwhelming concern for Narciso propelled Guadalupe to engage a local curandera, Cora, a mysterious Mexican Indian folk healer.

Reputed for her famous healing powers, a legend emerged about the spirit of her elder invoking her and granting Cora the magical healing secrets of the pagan past.

Guadalupe didn't care that the Catholic Church forbade such practices. She needed her husband to recover and believed that Haro's death and Raúl's departure were the beginning of Narciso's decline.

Cora created herbal formulas to heal Narciso's broken heart. She began with la limpia, a traditional cleansing ritual to help Narciso cope with the deaths of his beloved daughter and brother. Narciso seemed to rally for a while, but a nagging cough persisted, and he rapidly declined.

Two days later, a vaquero helped Narciso move onto a cot in the jacala that Guadalupe used as a steam room, and now filled with the medicinal scents of eucalyptus.

"I'll be around to guide my sons to manhood," he whispered hoarsely to Guadalupe, who held his head on her lap. The room was hot and steamy, with the curative vapers overwhelming the small enclosure.

"Get well, mi Amor," she whispered, "my love."

"I can't complain, can I, mi Cariña," his voice weakened from whooping cough. "All my dreams came true with you and me together until the end." He began coughing, which shook his entire body.

Guadalupe's eyes pleaded with Cora, who prepared a hot tea made from the leaves of yerba buena, the mint plant growing in the garden. Guadalupe helped Narciso drink, and Cora began a low chant. Guadalupe kept vigil day and night. She brought the children to Narciso's bedside and led them in praying the rosary. Narciso lay still, his chest heaving as if struggling to breathe. He woke briefly and asked each of his children to hug him. One by one, each child took turns hugging their father—the oldest, twelve-year-old Jorge, got the tightest hug. Next came eleven-year-old Maria Clara, followed by ten-year-old José Blas and Maria Teresa. With each embrace for eight-year-old José Lino, seven-year-old Juan Nepomuceno, and four-year-old José Maria, Narciso weakened until he slipped into unconsciousness.

That night, the air was cold and crisp as Guadalupe walked the children to the house and asked that they watch over each other; she had to be with their Papá. Two women shivering in the cold told Guadalupe they would stay the night to comfort the bewildered children. Even twelve-year-old Jorge, the eldest, couldn't comprehend the seriousness of their father's illness.

Later, another vaquero stopped by the jacala, and Guadalupe asked that he bring her a chair on which she could lean back. Narciso began to moan in delirium, and she leaned over to kiss his forehead. His skin was alarmingly hot, and she called out to Cora.

"We have to cool him down," Cora declared. She left the jacala carrying clean sheets. When she returned, she placed the wet linen over Narciso, calming him. Late into the night, Guadalupe heard Cora chanting softly. She again pressed her face onto Narciso's hot one and whispered, "Don't leave me, mi Amor." She wrapped herself in a shawl and fell asleep on the chair.

She sat up with a jerk; the baby's kick had awakened her. She looked up and saw Cora standing close by. "El Don ha pasado al otro lado," she said simply.

Narciso had passed to the other side. El Agostadero de San Juan de Carricitos had lost its greatest advocate.

Epilogue

TO UNFORGIVING HISTORY, IT ABANDONS A NAME, INDIFFERENT AND UNCONCERNED WHETHER IT DIE OR WHETHER IT ENDURE.

~MANUEL ACUÑA BEFORE A CORPSE [12]

Guadalupe buried Narciso in his beloved San Juan de Carricitos. He was fifty-two years old. The following month, in January 1803, when she was twenty-nine, Guadalupe delivered a girl, Rosalia.

Genealogical records show that Guadalupe lived to the age of seventy-four when she died in 1847, but do not indicate her place of death nor burial site, nor do they state that she remarried. Likely, not. However, in 1803, Guadalupe had eight children, ranging in age from a newborn to the oldest boy of twelve. She must have been a woman of strength and endurance as the person now in charge of San Juan de Carricitos. If she continued with Narciso's dream of building a township, she must oversee all aspects of completing a hacienda for her family; in order to name the town, she would need three hundred families to commit to remain.

We don't know how destructive the Native American attacks were, nor how often they persisted. Did Guadalupe have the protection of Narciso's family and the community to help her through those grim times and her vulnerable condition? For other pioneers struggling to solidify their land ownership parcel, how much time could individual owners lose assisting Guadalupe to hold on to the Agostadero? Perhaps she had enough and longed for the genteel life of her past, one without the worry or concern of Indian attacks.

What is known is that Native American tribes drove off the principal families in 1811. Not knowing the names of those who left, we can conjecture that Guadalupe decided to leave El Agostadero with her children to a safer haven, possibly her parents' home in Nuevo Leon. Despite this, the Agostadero was never permanently abandoned.

Juan Narciso Cavazos, Narciso's grandson, withstood his hold on the Agostadero when Narciso's and Guadalupe's sons, José Jorge, and Juan Nepomuceno, wanted to sell off some of the lands. Juan Narciso's father, Manuel, was Narciso's and Maria Ignacia's eldest son and the sole heir to the property, according to Spanish custom. Perhaps these younger Cavazos' sensed a bad outcome. They came of age in a battle-weary era of Mexican wars with France, Spain, and the Colonies of America, whose inhabitants continued encroaching upon the Mexican Texans' lands.

During the second decade of 1800, tensions escalated in the U.S. over slavery, economy, and state rights. Mexico began to undermine Spain's control over its central government. Spanish hacienda owners faced assaults from Mexico's peasant class, who, too, wanted the return of their land and battled for change against the caste-like systems that gripped Mexico. It's possible that landowners, like Narciso's descendants in Texas, wanted Mexico emancipated from Spanish control and allied with the United States. Mexican officials, no longer seeking clearance from Spain, once again opened settlements in Texas.

When the United States had its first significant economic crisis, the Panic of 1819, it spurred American citizens to emigrate to the Mexican states of Coahuila and Texas. [13]

In Alabama, for example, failed banks, property foreclosures, and the decline in the price of its main export, cotton, caused thousands of families to search for a fresh start in Texas.

In 1820, Mexico won independence from Spain, which left it without local industry or funds. Texas, mainly comprised of Mexican-born residents, needed Mexico to defend against the furor of Indian attacks along deserted stretches of Texas towns outside the San Antonio presidios. A provincial council convened to address this problem which also affected the Anglo settlers moving into Texas, who encountered similar clashes with Indians. Meanwhile, the tumult and intrigue of Mexican revolutionaries turned Texas into a hotbed for adventurers, traders, outlaws, and fortune seekers looking to hatch schemes of forming personal empires. Alarmed at the prospect of losing control of Texas, a new Mexican Commission on Foreign Relations issued the immigration of Irish and Germans to settle into the fertile lands of Texas to prevent the United States from annexing Texas and the Mexican states bordering the Rio Grande River. This decree brought Moses Austin of Missouri, along with his son, Stephen, both familiar with Spanish law and the language, to settle three hundred colonists on 200,000 acres of land near San Antonio. Today, Austin is the state capital of Texas. What might Narciso have accomplished with three hundred colonists and their families?

Mexico's encouragement of foreign settlements motivated the U.S. National Congress to decree land contracts in Texas. [14] The purpose of the law was "to augment the settlement of Texas territory, to advance the raising and increase of stock...in regions east of the Rio Grande." According to the terms, "soldiers and native Mexicans" were the preferred colonists. With Spanish being the primary language in Texas and with a law subject to interpretation, it is no wonder that this ruling adversely affected Mexican Texans.

Colonization eventually proved unfavorable to the Cavazos. Acquiring such a gargantuan parcel of land, Narciso and the other Cavazos owners had insufficient reinforcements. The land granted to Narciso was initially deemed "uninhabitable," a "no man's land" by both Mexico and Spain, which likely prevented Narciso from attracting settlers. Narciso had an attractive pedigree as a descendant of King Ferdinand III of Castile Spain. Perhaps he was given the Agostadero due to this bloodline.

Narciso spent at least two decades writing letters to the King of Spain for the same opportunity his ancestors experienced to explore the frontier of Texas. Perhaps he was given this so-called forsaken territory to keep him occupied. Narciso started from the beginning—by clearing the land, building quarters, planting fields and orchards, and digging wells and acequias. The community had to grow their food and tend to the large stock grazing the pasture. One must picture the physical strength and stamina necessary to make measurable progress. A more extensive census would have made appreciable headway in accomplishing the demands Spain imposed—a town or village with a hacienda, a gathering hall, dwellings for the pioneers, and a church—within five years of his occupation. Securing the land required fencing, which did not occur in the late 1700s. A Spaniard like Narciso most likely didn't frighten easily during Indian attacks or when encountering squatters appropriating property. With more hands, however, Narciso would have had vaqueros to scout the premises, protect property from Indian attacks, and, to prevent theft, help brand the animals that flourished on the rich pasture. In Cavazos' last will, 5000 heads of unbranded cattle alone occupied the Agostadero range. Narciso's pioneers permanently settled only a fraction of the acreage. Narciso did not name any of the lands as townships, perhaps he intended to keep the original name given by Spain, El Agostadero de San Juan de Carricitos to his town. Consequently, before 1836, the Cavazos families risked forfeiting it back to the Mexican government.

The U. S. admitted Texas as the twenty-eighth state in 1845 and began a series of pre-emption grants, later called the Homestead Act of 1854. People who settled on public land could purchase up to 320 acres allowing Americans already "squatting" the impetus to move in on Mexican claims. Many Mexican landowners, unfamiliar with the American legal system, lost their property. New local authorities began to invalidate an abundance of land claims. Authentic documents from centuries-old claims handed in good faith to court officers were lost, stolen, or forged.

In 1842, my great-great-grandfather, Antonio Cavazos, lived five miles east of Hidalgo, near Rancho Edinburg (Hidalgo) and Pharr, on a 5535-acre tract that now is the Jackson-Brewster Ranch bordering the northern bank of the Rio Grande River. The property was on a river frontage of seven-tenths of a mile that extended thirteen miles north between the present cities of Pharr and San Juan. Antonio Cavazos sold the northern part of his ranch, porción 71, to E.D. Smith. Years later, Antonio died on the Jackson Ranch by accidental drowning. My family has been unsuccessful in recovering the documentation for this transaction.

During the first United States census in 1850, taken in what is now the state of Texas, my great-grandparents, Ysidoro Cavazos,[15] and Estefana Sanchez, [16] were living in Edinburg, Texas, with their respective parents. In 1857, E.D. Smith sold Antonio Cavazos' former Spanish Land Grant ranch to Nathaniel Jackson for thirty- six cents an acre.

Jackson was a loyal Unionist during the Civil War who left Alabama in 1857. Jackson and his African American wife Matilda Hicks, his son Eli, and other adult children hoped to escape the intolerance of interracial marriage they had known in the South. Accompanying the Jacksons were eleven African American freedmen. Today, this land is valued at $413.4M.

In the History of Raymondville and Willacy County,[17] Nola Martin Harding writes that the land Narciso received was oftentimes referred to as La Laguna del Perdido, the Lost Lagoon, which denoted "a man either was lost or died in the area." Narciso would not be the last Cavazos to die in lands that were once San Juan de Carricitos.

During the COVID-19 pandemic, a series of articles appeared in journals regarding the land of Fred Cavazos. The Trump administration sought to seize his land, which Cavazos described as "home since before it was the United States." The long-awaited southern border wall, promised by Trump, cut directly through Mr. Cavazos' property. [18]

Today, Narciso's land is part of the Jackson-Brewster Ranch and the King Ranch. Richard King acquired the property in 1853, and his ranch is acclaimed as The Birthplace of American Ranching. There is some irony to a King owning the Agostadero. However, the source of cattle ranching in Texas began with a land grant from the King of Spain in 1792.

Narciso's beneficiaries fought hard to maintain his legacy. Court documents record the legal struggle pursued by heirs. As late as 1889, the descendants filed a two-by-five-foot hand-printed "Family Tree" of José Narciso in the District Court of Cameron County in the "Richard King versus the (sixty-seven) Heirs and Assigns of Narciso Cavazos." Nola Martin Harding writes that the case involved "partitioning the San Juan de Carricitos Grant between the owners of record,"[19] which included Richard King!

The court decided a parcel of land to each owner comprising the acreage "to which he was entitled." In 1889, a parcel was equivalent to forty acres. Narciso's nine children each received one ninth of the divided property.

Narciso's adopted son, José Lino, inherited La Hacienda De Los Cavazos in Nuevo Leon, Mexico, the setting for this story. My father was born there in 1898. As children, we visited the Hacienda, which remained in the family until 2000.

The gateway ancestors Narciso and I descended from are Captain Juan Cavazos del Campo (1605-1683) and Elena De La Garza Rodriguez (1607-1705) from Castilla, Spain, who, after their marriage in 1627, came to Monterrey, Nuevo Leon, Mexico.

Texas is the birthplace of the Cavazos name, the longhorn cattle, the vaquero cowboy, and, along with the other Grantees given Texas land by the King of Spain, gave rise to the Tejanos of today. A plaque in Sebastian, Texas, mentions San Juan de Carricitos.

Originally part of the San Juan de Carricitos Land Grant. This townsite later was part of South Texas's famed King Ranch. Sebastian was known as Stillman Town Tract until 1906 when it was renamed to honor an officer of the Rock Island Railroad. In 1914 The Sebastian Realty Company was promoting the town in the hope that it would become a major agricultural center. During the early 20th Century period of lawlessness in South Texas, Sebastian experienced a bandit raid in which two members of the Austin Family were killed.

Another plaque in Raymondville describes more of its history:

The largest land grant in South Texas, the San Juan de Carricitos landswere (sic) awarded to Don Jose Narciso Cavazos in 1792 by the King of Spain.

Comprising over one-half million acres, the grant included virtually all of present Willacy County, including the sites of the towns of Sebastian, Lyford, Raymondville, Lasara, San Perlita, and Port Mansfield. In 1793 Cavazos took formal possession of the land grant seven miles north of this site. Most of the grant was later sold by Cavazos' heirs, although some descendants still live within its boundaries.

Narciso's dream of acres and acres of land and his drive to pursue it at all costs launched the beginning Texas history. I began writing this ancestral memoir in October 2018. I based this narrative on verified events—and family legend storytelling. I collected an extensive bibliography of books, abstracts, web pages, and videos.

Without Narciso, none of his descendants would have realized growing up Texan. I recognize Narciso as one of my ancestors whose strength, determination, and tenacity allowed him to adjust to formidable forces—he either adapted strategies to cultivate and preserve his colossal property or capitulate. He died before he completed the requirements imposed by Spain. Still, I credit him for his investment in family, ranching, farming, town settlement, and preserving the rich cultural history that shaped and tamed a wild frontier. His legacy as a pioneer merged the vibrant mores of the assimilated Indian, Mexican, and Spanish way of life. Future generations continued in the regions of San Juan de Carricitos as the land changed and grew into townships and boroughs, then towns and cities. Since Texas became her own country, then part of the United States, for 230 years, her people have forever seen themselves not as Indian, Mexican, or Spanish but as Tejanos. They continue to instill strong family values, including cultural loyalty and Catholicism. The Tejano culture adapts well to the conditions of the regions they occupy. The people on both sides of the border share a common interest unique to this heritage. Future generations are bilingual and continue to speak English as well as the native language of Spain. I am proud of my Spanish Mexican heritage as a descendant of the First Families of Bexar County through my paternal ancestors and as a descendant of El Cid on my maternal side.

More thorough and complete research on this most exciting ancestor, José Narciso Cavazos, will claim this Texas pioneer and trailblazer his rightful place in history. He deserves the designation as one of the forerunners of Texas ranching history. I'm hoping that my extensive bibliography may someday encourage further scholarship in one of many Spanish ancestors who, beginning with the conquistadors in 1598 and along with the Indian, Spanish, and Mexican people changed Texas in numerous ways, to make it the Texas of today.

Auntie didn't find her baptismal certificate on this trip. Will that stop her from looking for it?

El Fin

Endnotes:

[1] 1924, August 24. Missing Boy Drowned. Recovery of body ends rumor of barrel murder. The New York Times

[2] Engageantes are false sleeves worn with women's clothing.

[3] The grant, 601,657 acres, included virtually all of present-day Willacy County, including the sites of the towns of Sebastian, Lyford, Raymondville, Lasara, San Perlita, and Port Mansfield.

[4] Divide the area (600,000 acres) by 7628 (square nautical leagues) for an approximation of a league.

[5] A hut with a thatched roof and walls consisting of mud plastered over thin stakes driven into the ground.

[6] The first Spanish fort Presidio La Bahía built in 1722 in what is now Goliad Texas.

[7] San Antonio de Béxar Presidio was founded by Martín de Alarcón on May 5, 1718, on the San Antonio River.

[8] Espíritu Santo to José Salvador de la Garza in 1781, Concepción de Cerritos to Bartolomé de la Garza in 1789, Llano Rancho to Juan José Hinojosa and La Feria Rancho to José Mari

Balli; both in 1790.

[9] The Church's position that first cousins are forbidden to marry only by ecclesiastical law, not by divine law. For this reason, it is canonically possible to receive a dispensation that permits

two first cousins to marry validly in the Catholic Church. (This assumes, of course, that it is legal under civil law in the area where the marriage is to take place.)

[10] A freshwater wetland is highly acidic, soft, spongy, and cold, with low- oxygen levels making it ideal for preservation.

[11] According to a Google search, the term African American has crept steadily into the nation's vocabulary since **1988** when the Rev. Jesse

Jackson held a news conference to

Urge Americans to use it to refer to Blacks. "It puts us in our proper historical context…"

12 Paz, Octavio. (1985) *Mexican Poetry: An Anthology.* Translated by Samuel Beckett. New York: Grove Press, Inc.

13 Later the Republic of Texas in 1836, and later still the U.S. State of Texas in 1845.

14 https://www.tshaonline.org/handbook/entries/mexican-colonization-laws

15 Parents Antonio Cavazos and Juana de la Peña

16 Parents Manuel Sanchez-Benavides and Maria-Josefa de la Garza Sosa

17 Sponsored by Valley By-Liners. *Gift of the Rio: Story of Texas' Tropical Borderland.* 1975. Border Kingdom Press, Mission Texas

18 Pacific Standard Magazine, October 2018; Texas Observer, January 2019; The New York Post, April 2019; The digital magazine, Reinventing Home, March 2020.

19 Ibid. Gift of the Rio: Story of Texas' Tropical Borderland.

About the Author

Bernadette Inclan is a multifaceted individual with professional and creative pursuits. From her Linkedin profiles, she has forty-five years' experience as a Cytotechnologist and is currently retired.

Bernadette is a member of the Arizona Authors Association (AAA); member and secretary to the Phoenix Writers Club, the oldest Writers club in Arizona and celebrating its centennial in 2026. She facilitates Phoenix Writers Club Critique Group (PWCCG) and Writers Inspiration Group (WIG).

Bernadette is also an author whose story, Time to Say Goodbye appeared in the Inkslingers Anthology Volume 5 Many Worlds Many Stories. Her book The Perils of Beginnings won the Phoenix Writers Club Uta Behrens award for non-fiction and has a five-star rating on Goodreads. She also maintains a Substack newsletter where she shares thoughts, stories, and memoirs. Additionally, she has an Instagram account.

Bernadette was born and raised in Galveston Texas graduating from the historical all girls' school, Ursuline Academy. She attended colleges in the San Antonio area, Incarnate Word College (now The University of the Incarnate Word), and the University of Texas at San Antonio where she earned a bachelor's degree and ASCP Board Certification in Cytotechnology at the University of Texas Medical School. Graduate studies in Health Care Management at Southwest Texas University (now Texas State University), and a promotion to Regional Cytology Manager moved her to San Diego CA, then Phoenix AZ, where she now resides with her husband. Bernadette has two sons, a granddaughter, and two great-grandchildren.

www.ingramcontent.com/pod-product-compliance
Lightning Source LLC
Chambersburg PA
CBHW071726120626
46550CB00002B/401